Crossing Borders

Crossing Borders

Changing Social Identities in Southern Mexico

Kimberly M. Grimes

The University of Arizona Press
Tucson

The University of Arizona Press
© 1998 The Arizona Board of Regents
First Printing
All rights reserved

♾ This book is printed on acid-free, archival-quality paper.
Manufactured in the United States of America

03 02 01 00 99 98   6   5   4   3   2   1

Library of Congress Cataloging-in-Publication Data
Grimes, Kimberly M., 1961–
    Crossing borders : changing social identities in southern
Mexico / Kimberly M. Grimes.
    p. cm.
  Includes bibliographical references and index.
  ISBN 0-8165-1716-9 (acid-free paper)
  ISBN 0-8165-1707-2 (pbk. : acid-free paper)
    1. Putla de Guerrero (Mexico)—Emigration and immigration. 2.
Putla de Guerrero (Mexico)—Social conditions. 3. Emigrant
remittances—Mexico—Putla de Guerrero. 4. United
States—Emigration and immigration. 1. Title.
    JV7409.P47 G74 1998
    325'.27274—ddc21   97-45411
                          CIP

British Library Cataloguing-in-Publication Data
A catalogue record for this book is available from the British Library.

For Marco

Contents

Figures

Acknowledgments

i want to first thank the people of Putla and the Putlecans in Mexico City and Atlantic City, New Jersey, who benevolently shared their knowledge, their time, and their hospitality with me. To them I owe the greatest debt, for without their support and collaboration this book would never have been written. I especially want to thank Sra. Amparo Aguilar and the entire Santiago Aguilar family for giving us a home in Putla and for always being there whenever I needed help.

I thank the people of the Centro de Investigaciones y Estudios Superiores de Antropología Social (CIESAS) in Oaxaca for their support. Special thanks go to Salomón Nahmad Sitton, who generously shared his knowledge of Oaxaca with me and who directed me to archival sources in Oaxaca City. I thank the University of Arizona's Department of Anthropology for the Comins Fellowship, which provided initial support for my research. I want to extend a special thank you to James Greenberg, Ana Alonso, and Jane Hill for their advice, insights, and criticisms of this work.

I want to express my deepest gratitude to the people at the Bureau of Applied Research in Anthropology at the University of Arizona and especially the director, Timothy Finan, for the intellectual, financial, and emotional support that sustained me from the beginning of my research to the final phase of writing. I also want to thank Marcela Vásquez, Anita Wood, Catherine Tucker, and Jacqueline Messing for their suggestions and encouragement.

Jorge Mendoza combined the various neighborhood maps from the tax office in Putla to make figure 2.1, and I thank him for his work. I also want to thank Susan Jorstad, who drew figure 1.1 and reduced figure 2.1. I thank the Instituto Nacional de Antropología e Historia (INAH) in Mexico City for granting me permission to reprint figure 2.2. Mapping Specialists, Ltd., in Madison, Wisconsin, produced the final copy of all three maps, and I thank them for doing such a wonderful job.

I want to thank the anonymous reviewers and my editor, Chris Szuter, for their comments and corrections and for helping me to reorganize sections of this book.

I would like to express special thanks also to Alison Smith for her help.

My in-laws, Elena Aguilar and Filadelfo Hernández, introduced me to Putla with their childhood stories and have continued helping me with my research to this day. I can never thank them enough for all the love and kindness they have given me. The same is true for my family, especially my mother, Sandra Robertson, and my sister, Rebecca Mais. I'm blessed to have such wonderful people in my life.

Finally, I owe my most profound debt to Marco Hernández. Marco has been by my side throughout this project, providing encouragement and love. He continuously shared his knowledge about Mexico with me, and his observations and insights helped me to rethink many first impressions and to better understand people's thoughts and actions in Putla, in Mexico, and in the United States. His contributions are evident throughout this book.

Crossing Borders

1
Introduction

The most interesting and difficult part of any cultural analysis, in complex societies, is that which seeks to grasp the hegemonic in its active and formative but also its transformational processes.

(R. Williams 1977:113)

i sit watching the bustle of people getting ready to board the bus. Families kiss and hug their kin good-bye, giving last-minute advice and instructions. Children run around as their mothers yell to them to get out of the road. Men heave burlap sacks filled with dried chiles to the driver on top of the bus. Young men joke and punch each other, hiding their uneasiness as they begin their first trip to *el norte*. Soon everyone is onboard, and the bus belches smoke and rumbles off. The trip up the windy mountain road begins.

Living next to the bus terminal in a western Oaxacan town for more than a year, I observed this daily bus-filling ritual hundreds of times. Yet each time was new, exciting. I could feel the strong emotion from the people leaving and from those saying their farewells. It made me reflect upon all the articles and books that I had read on migration before arriving there to do my research. I felt disappointed. How could so much be written on the subject of migration yet so little capture what it means to the people who experience it and their families, their friends, their community?

At the same time, I felt intimidated and overwhelmed. I had come there to understand how migration had changed and was changing life in a town in Mexico. Obviously I knew there would be no clear-cut answer. Different personal histories and experiences formed in different contexts and with different historical consciousnesses would generate a multitude of changes—some quite evident, others more subtle. It was this variation that I was after. But I wondered if in a town where some 20,000 people lived it would be possible to capture, understand, and interpret the social change occurring and the role migration played. Thus I began my journey into the lives of the people of Putla de Guerrero: Putla from the Aztec name Pochtlán, meaning "place of fog." The name comforted me as it came to symbolize my entry into a community that I knew somewhat and my position within the community as neither insider nor outsider.

Telling the Story

Doing anthropological research these days is like trying to walk along the top of a fence, always tipping from one side to the other, looking for a way to re-present people's lives without resorting to academic imperialism. Recognizing past errors of asserting authoritative claims about the "other" has led to a questioning of the anthropologist's role and goals in anthropological research. My uneasiness as a white, U.S. academic studying the lives of a group of people in Oaxaca was heightened by the requirements of academia as to what was acceptable and necessary for scholarly research. Conscious of my particular subject position, I tried to mitigate my uneasiness by not silencing other voices and by selecting a research area in which I have a strong personal as well as professional interest. For years I had listened to stories that my in-laws would tell about "el pueblo"—a nameless town in Oaxaca near the state of Guerrero. One born in Putla and the other in a town near Putla, my in-laws were part of the mass rural exodus to the Federal District in the late 1950s. My husband, born and raised in Mexico City, had visited Putla when he was young but knew little about the place of his ancestors. I wanted to learn more about the place, its history, its people—not just for my research but for our future children. Living in Putla did not make me a Putlecan, yet I was not an absolute outsider because of my family ties.

I believe that my family connection made me more responsible to the people because it increased my awareness of how my research could affect their lives. I knew that families did not discuss certain problems outside the home. People worried about their reputations and the local gossip that could result if they discussed these subjects with me or if they spoke harshly about others in the community. More than anything else, money was a taboo subject. When asking questions about money, such as how much a family member had sent from the United States, most people would answer *un poco* (a little) even when they had built a two-story house with indoor plumbing and set up a small business with the remittances. Putlecans eagerly display new wealth through the purchase of consumer items, but they consider it in bad taste to speak about money or, worse, to boast about it.[1] I never pushed people for information when they hesitated to answer or seemed uncomfortable. Rather, I would quickly change the conversation, the way my family members did when conversations became too personal. Remembering, too, that I could harm my family's reputation made me conform more to local etiquette.

I do not want to give the impression that I felt in any way restricted due to my family connection; I simply felt more responsible and in tune with the community's members. Moreover, many times my research was aided by this connection. Some people who were at first suspicious of why a *gringa* wanted to know about their family relaxed when they learned that I was married to a man whose family was originally from Putla. That information helped to assure people that I was not another North American evangelist or a CIA spy investigating undocumented Putlecans in the United States.

With time, however, I came to realize that my acceptance in the community had as much to do with migration processes as with my family. Almost every family with whom I visited had a family member or members living in the United States. Without intending to, the gringa became the source for information about the United States, and my voice "the authority." Most of the time I enjoyed answering peoples' questions, even the uncomfortable ones, such as if it is true that the U.S. government does not consider parents dependents and thus will not allow children to send money home to their parents. Questions like this one placed me in the middle of family tensions that had resulted from sons or daughters not sending money as they had been expected to do. But I learned more from many of these discussions than I did from the questions I had prepared. What made me anxious, however, was the belief that I knew more than the Putlecans did because I was a *norteamericana* (white, female, U.S. citizen). Many Putlecans believe that all white people in the United States are intelligent, well-educated, kind, clean, and altruistic—"they even stop for animals in the road." These beliefs are something that I will discuss in greater detail later on, but it suffices to say now that they constructed my identity in ways that I found unsettling. Looking back at it now I can see the irony in the situation—what anthropologists have been doing to the "other" for years was now being done to one of them by the "other."

I remember one day when I went to the post office to pick up a package my sister had sent me. Several days before, I had interviewed the postman's sister and they had obviously talked about me and my research. Always polite, he asked if I would tell him a bit more about the purpose of my research. I explained my interest in the town and in its history. He smiled as he told me that he was very happy to have a North American, rather than a fellow townsperson, writing his town's history. He explained that the people in Putla were ignorant of and uninterested in their own *raíces* (cultural roots). Nor, he remarked, does the Mexican government care about the townspeople, because politicians are *corruptos* (corrupt, spoiled). Only "foreigners" (referring to U.S. citizens or Europeans) care enough to come and to write "our" history, he noted. He was paying me a compliment, but I felt uncomfortable with the insinuation that foreigners were somehow "superior" and more altruistic than Mexican people.

I did not have to pay my dues so to speak to earn my status; the townspeople gave me the voice of authority. It is interesting to compare my easy entry into the community with my husband's. Even though it was my husband's relatives who were from Putla, he had problems in the beginning with young men wanting to pick a fight with him because he was *chilango*.[2] The young men expressed the resentment, frustration, and jealousy felt by many rural Mexicans toward people from the nation's capital. My husband had to earn respect in the town, which he accomplished rather quickly through teaching English classes and playing music in La Casa de la Cultura. His students admired him, and word passed rapidly that he was *buena onda* (a good person).

I also realized that more than just being accorded "authority" I was treated as a commodity and engaged as a status symbol by "middle-class" people in the town, mainly younger Putlecans who had studied a career in Mexico City or Oaxaca City and who were striving for greater "whiteness."[3] The gringa and her husband were invited to all the "uptown" social events, where at times I felt like a dressed-up mannequin, a form representing a human figure, something to be seen with—not someone you talk to. Once at a party given by my husband's aunt (in Anglo kinship, she would be called a cousin), the aunt took me by the hand with my husband following behind and introduced me to her friends table by table as "mi sobrina y su esposo" (my niece and her husband). We never stopped to engage in a conversation with any of these people and by the end of the tour, I was seated by her side at the head table.

My personal experiences made me comprehend how much power relations affect and are affected by the process of research. My relationship with the community was constantly being reshaped and redefined as we all struggled to understand one another.

The Research Process

Although the field of cultural anthropology is undergoing a critical reassessment of roles and goals, one stable or defining element is its commitment to participant observation; cultural anthropologists live with the people they study in communities throughout the world. The information that informs this study comes from living in Putla for three months in 1991, ten months in 1993, and four months in 1994; in Mexico City for varying amounts of time from 1989 to today; and in Atlantic City,[4] New Jersey, for three weeks in 1994. I also made several day trips to other communities in the region in order to understand Putla's position as *cabecera* (county seat) of the district.

Putla is a medium-sized community in the mountains of western Oaxaca—a community that is located in one of the economically poorest regions in Mexico today (figure 1.1). Members of the town have a long tradition of migration to Mexican urban centers and to the United States, and a high out-migration rate. Because one of the main goals of my research was to understand the relationship between circular migration and the reconstruction of social identities and social relations, I needed to grasp the heterogeneity of the town's peoples. Due to time and money constraints, I could not interview everyone in the town to determine its social makeup, so I selected a random sample. I interviewed at least one member of 378 families, the sample size required for a population of 20,000 (Bernard 1988:105). During many of the interviews, everyone who was home at the time became curious and joined in the conversations. The formal questionnaire consisted of 134 questions covering a wide range of issues: family relations; education; leisure time; economic, political, and religious activities; personal aspirations and aversions; and migration histories of family members (see appendix). Many questions were open ended, which led to extended conversations on many of the topics.

From the group of people that I interviewed, I selected thirty-three women and men of different ages, classes, and marital statuses and recorded their life histories in order to understand how the experi-

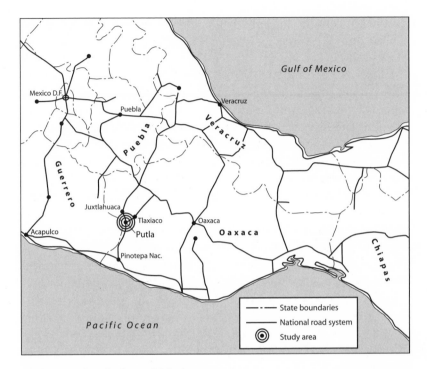

Figure 1.1. South-Central Mexico

ences—and conceptions of self and others—of community members who had migrated differed from those who had not. In telling their own life histories, women and men revealed that social identity is never static. People actively construct, modify, defend, and challenge conceptions of the self and of social position within the family, the local community, the nation-state, and the international community.

Some of the Putlecans' responses and concerns led me to examine attitudes and practices I had not previously considered. For example, not until I joined the local ecology group did I fully comprehend the profound impact that consumption processes have on a community.[5] The research was a feedback process. As I learned from the people of Putla and they from me, our repertoires of questions expanded and, in many instances, included areas of mutual concern.

Little historical or anthropological-sociological research has been conducted specifically on the region of Putla. I reviewed colonial, nineteenth-century, and twentieth-century documents relating to the Putla region in the Archivo General de la Nación (National Archives) in Mexico City, in two state archives in Oaxaca City (Archivo General del Estado de Oaxaca and Archivo General de Notaría y Registro Público de la Propiedad), and in the Catholic Church archive in Putla in order to understand the community's history and the broader national and international historical processes that have affected the region.[6] As Gmelch (1980:135) points out, many studies of migration have tended to view migration as a "static event" due to the nature of traditional anthropological fieldwork; researchers live for a limited time in a limited space. My study brings a diachronic perspective to migration studies and focuses on the relational aspects of experience, knowledge, and productive activities.

This study seeks to understand how migration and social change shape and are shaped by people and practices in specific historical moments interacting dialectically with broader social, economic, and political structures. My study views women and men as "actors"— people who make choices and who critically understand their positions. One of the contributions of this study is its attention to specifics. Though my research addresses questions of broad relevance, it does so by focusing on the quotidian and on the choices people make as they go about their daily lives. I examine gender, "race," ethnicity, age, class, sexuality, marital status, and position within the family as crucial markers in processes of social differentiation and in the social reproduction of gender-racial-class hierarchies in which women and men are situated. Focusing on the multiple axes of identity and agency allows me to understand the often conflictual and contradictory character of people's lives. My research uses the concept of hegemony to demonstrate that power is not separate from meaning. The social construction of common meanings plays an important role in the creation of consent, collaboration, or resistance.

Studies of Migration

Over the past thirty years, the literature examining migration has rapidly multiplied, making it a central concern in the social sciences and in law (S. Tomasi, L. Tomasi, and Miller 1989). Witnessing the mass rural exodus within and the rapid urbanization of most "third" world countries following World War II and the steady growth of international migration, researchers have focused on understanding the causes of migration and have prioritized economics in the investigations. Four main perspectives have emerged in the literature: neoclassical economic approaches, structural-historical approaches, studies that focus on the household as the basic unit of analysis, and studies that examine migrants' social networks.[7]

Each of these approaches has provided many insights about migration. No one can deny that the gap in employment possibilities and wages between sending and receiving areas worldwide spur many people to migrate. Such is the case in rural Oaxaca, where many people lack adequate land or water or both to farm, or capital to start a business. Day labor will not feed the family, so they leave. Structural-historical models demonstrate the importance of relating regional migration patterns to the broader socioeconomic and political transformations within nations and in the international community. The link between capitalist expansion and expanded migration is critical to our understanding of current migration patterns. For example, Cornelius (1988) identifies macrolevel factors in both the Mexican and the U.S. economies that played a central role in Mexican migration to its northern neighbor in the 1980s: the automation and fragmentation of manufacturing production globally; the expansion of service industries in the United States; the increasing employer preference for part-time, temporary workers; the changing U.S. demographic profile; and the negative or negligible economic growth in Mexico since the 1982 economic crisis.

Household studies show that migration is often a collective sustenance strategy employed by its members to ensure its maintenance and reproduction. In many rural areas in Mexico, including those in Oaxaca, families are supported by remittances sent from members working in cities or in the United States. Without these remittances, many families could not remain in the countryside. Social networks link family and community members in receiving and sending communities, providing some security to migrants, who are often vulnerable in the new setting. These social network studies also examine migration as a long-term process, overcoming the problem of treating migration as a static event.

With each of these approaches, however, something is still missing. Repetitive descriptions of economic push-pull factors suffer from a timeless functionality, and people do not mechanically respond to structural factors. If they did, everyone living in marginalized, impoverished areas in the world should have already migrated. We need to look at other aspects of people's lives, rather than focus narrowly on the economic, in order to understand the diversity of human agency.

Household studies try to connect individual behavior with larger economic and political processes, but they assume that households are homogenous. The social actors are invisible. A household "chooses" migration when it can no longer maintain its desired consumption level and decides the advantages of migration outweigh its costs (Bach and Schraml 1982:332–333). These studies imply a collective rationality (rather than individual rationality) in decision making. But households do not "choose"; people do. The concept is reified.

Moreover, the view of households as undifferentiated units, sites of sharing and cooperation, fails to recognize intrafamily relations in which gender hierarchies and other relations of domination and exploitation are constructed.[8] Especially in Latin America, focus on the household has led scholars to underestimate "the autonomous role played by kin structures in regulating social life" (Grasmuck 1991:2). Mexican scholars argue that the extended family is the "basic meaningful unit of solidarity in Mexico" (Lomnitz and Pérez-Lizaur 1987:7; Warman 1980). The extended family plays a greater role in the lives of Mexicans than is seen in studies using the household as their basic unit of analysis. Lastly, although examination of the life cycles of migrants' social networks has vastly improved our understandings of migrant communities, network studies (like household studies) have also "unwittingly masked the power of gender in shaping migration" (Hondagneu-Sotelo 1994:6–7, 53–97).

Knowledge, Power, and Migration

The general perspectives that guide mainstream migration studies fall short of grasping the diverse experiences and histories of the people who migrate, the differing political and economic contexts from which they embark, and the transformations migration generates in their personal lives and in the communities in which they live. In 1989, editors of the *International Migration Review* assessed a quarter-century of migration research and concluded that "scholarship on international migration is still searching for a general theory capable of elucidating the multiple facets of the complex drama involved in international migration" (S. Tomasi, L. Tomasi, and Miller 1989:396). The review highlighted important areas of research missing from migration studies—such as lack of attention paid to the role of the state, the deficiency of information on "third" world nations, the need for contextualization of migration as a global phenomenon, and the demand for raising ethical questions of state immigration policies— unexamined assumptions still undermine much of the scholarly research on migration.

Scholars hold on to the search for a totalizing theory to explain migration patterns and to direct policy strategies. "As a result, governmental policies now stand a much better chance of being informed by scientific research on international migration" (S. Tomasi, L. Tomasi, and Miller 1989:398). From this perspective, migrants become numbers to be counted, numbers that are to inform "first" world governmental policies. Because these studies are policy driven, they often serve the interests of states. Failing to address how hidden dominant ideologies have colored perceptions of migration remains a key problem in migration studies.

Understanding how knowledge is produced is key to liberating discourses on migration and social change from states' hegemonic agendas. By paying close attention to how we construct our subjects, we can challenge the dualisms and essentialism that pervade the migration literature. The manipulation of social identity by naturalizing and normalizing differences is a key strategy in the legitimization of economic and political domination (Gramsci 1971; R. Williams 1977). It produces ideological justifications that make domination the "natural" outcome of differences between women and men, of people of color and whites, and of poor people and the affluent. Differences are reduced to the simplicity of essences upon which dualist oppositions are built.

In development and migration literatures, the "third" world is constructed as traditional, poor, colored, led by emotions and feelings, feminine, whereas the "first" world is modern, wealthy, white, led by rational thought, masculine. The interrelationship of racial, class, and gender ideologies subordinates the "third" world in relation to the "first." By engendering the "third" world as feminine, "she" becomes irrational, instinctual, and excluded. The rational, modern "first" world retains its power to make universal knowledge claims. As Donna Haraway reminds us, the claim of "objectivity is not about dis-engagement, but about mutual and usually unequal structuring" (1991:201). Ironically, migration patterns reveal just how inappropriate the "first" world–"third" world dichotomy is. With the massive influx of "third" world peoples into the "first" world, "contemporary definitions of the 'third world' can no longer have the same geographical contours and boundaries they had. . . . In the post-industrial world, systemic socioeconomic and ideological processes position the peoples of Africa, Asia, Latin America and the Middle East, as well as 'minority' populations (people of color) in the United States and Europe" (Mohanty 1991:2).

State projects and political ideologies work to standardize migration contexts and immigrant experiences. In the mid-1970s, a time of economic recession in the United States, members of the U.S. House of Representatives Subcommittee on Immigration, Citizenship, and International Law blamed undocumented migrants for the high unemployment rate and for burdening local tax resources.[9] The American "myth of opportunity" was used to "reify illegal aliens in order to deny difference, inequality and history" (Chock 1991:279). "The typical opportunity story centers on an immigrant whose arrival in America, desire for betterment, striving in adversity, and putting down of roots make him a `new man.' That is, he is the Promethean hero of his own story; the story erases his past, foreign cultural baggage, and restraining social ties. The telling of such stories focused the debate about illegal immigration on individuals . . . rather than on social structure, culture or history" (Chock 1991:281).

By comparing contemporary undocumented immigrants to an idealized version of past "individual" immigrants, congressional members eliminated any possibility for challenges to their construction of the situation. With unitary individualism at the heart of the ideology of the dominant social group, relations of difference are relegated to a lower status than that held by the expressive forms of the dominant ideology (Corrigan 1990:121–123). The passage of Proposition O, the English-only campaign in San Francisco (Woolard 1989), and of

California's Proposition 187 in 1994 demonstrates the effectiveness of naturalizing arguments. These arguments persuaded a majority of the citizens of California (including many liberals) that the propositions were necessary for the state's well-being.

Proposition 187 highlights how "scientific" research on migration is manipulated by government policies. Supporters of the proposition presented statistical evidence to promote their claim that undocumented immigrants drained state resources, conveniently overlooking all other evidence to the contrary.[10] Rather than "objectively" informing government policy, studies on immigration have been subjectively applied to achieve particular political agendas. A study by Durand and Massey shows that for fifty years congressional representatives have used studies to exaggerate the number of Mexican immigrants in the United States; the numbers are used for "party politics" (1992:10). Bustamante (1983a, 1983b) demonstrates how Mexican migrants have become the political scapegoat in times of increasing unemployment, even though these workers have filled specific labor shortages in the United States during these times. Portes and Rumbaut discuss how economists in testimonies before the U.S. Congress proliferate the perceptions that contemporary immigrants are low skilled and the quality of immigrant labor is continuing to decline despite the fact that "highly educated immigrants remain strongly represented at the top of the U.S. occupational pyramid" (1990:58).

Migration and Social Change

Recent scholarship has begun questioning and examining the intellectual inadequacies and false assumptions that underlie methods and models in social analyses. Many of the critiques have shown how epistemology has been flattened in such a way that the complex and multiple means by which people construct and experience social life are lost or ignored.[11] Yet these critiques have yet to influence mainstream migration perspectives and their descriptions of immigrant populations. Migration scholars still tend to see immigrant populations as bounded social groups, essentializing complex social identities and social processes. In order to develop a more adequate knowledge of the interrelationships of social identities, social relations, and global processes in migration studies, we need to recognize the heterogeneity and multiplicity of subjectivities and experiences that produce diverse cultural forms. My point is not simply academic. The information derived from studies of migration and immigrant populations has reproduced and reinforced racist, classist, and sexist ideologies, increasing intolerance and hatred in societies today. By defining people as "insiders" versus "outsiders" and by essentializing migrants, scholars contribute to this process and make the possibility of empowerment of others who are not white (whether they are migrants or citizens) more difficult. Everyone in a nation loses when they fail to see immigrants' contributions to the economic and cultural enrichment of their country (Pronk 1993; Portes and Rumbaut 1990:245–246).

Essentializing migrants is the heart of acculturation studies, the popular model for looking at migration and social change from the 1930s to the 1970s (Roseberry 1989:84–85)—a model that continues to be used by U.S. politicians and in our public education system today. Through the processes of assimilation, adaptation, and acculturation, the donor culture divests the receptor of its former culture while the receptor eagerly tries to become more like the first—or as Rosaldo more aptly calls the process "deculturation," "to become part of the culturally invisible mainstream" (1989:209). This process culminates in the United States as the renowned "melting pot." Acculturationists reify cultures and assume that the donor and receptor cultures are autonomous, without any consideration of power relations. History is denied to at least one of the cultures. If the donor had history, the receptor was given by the dominant group only a historical baseline. Ironically, if the idea of pluralism was discussed by the donor culture, it was viewed as the outcome of contact (Roseberry 1989:86).

Ignoring the "other's" history, flattening social processes and human identities to fixed forms, denying agency, and negating the role of power in cultural production have left studies of migration and social change hollow. Migrants do not simply assimilate foreign cultures' ideas and practices but rather reconstruct new identities in the context of mediating institutions that shape their strategies and choices (Lamphere 1992). "Culturally and socially they [migrants] are something new, and they must be understood on their own terms" (Turino

1993:249). New identities coupled with new cultural practices are continuously created, modified, and digested, not fixed and essential.

As we look to understand social change in Latin America, the tendency to see change as unidirectional and fixed (i.e., the Americanization or Westernization of Latin America) obscures the complex processes shaping social change.[12] The question becomes how to understand social change and living differences in a particular community in a Latin American country (such as Putla in Mexico) that is exposed to (or even bombarded by at times) North American–European ideas and material goods via global communications, trade, and the people themselves who cross borders, without resorting to homogenizing, totalizing, and essentializing people and the spaces in which they live.

Negotiating Identity and Power across Borders

The concept of hegemony is fundamental to the development of a framework for understanding migration. Examining hegemonic processes that are actively constituted, modified, defended, and challenged by social groups allows us to observe the creative agency of migrants and immigrant populations within certain social, cultural, and historical limits. The constant interplay among material production, sociopolitical institutions, and experience and consciousness creates a social field in which migrants develop and sustain multiple relations across political borders. The reconstruction of social identities actively emerges within this multinational context. Individuals leave their social groups and enter new ones that offer different modes of thought, experience, feeling, and action. Migrants accommodate, challenge, renegotiate, and resist these new modes.

Social change is a relational process—a redefining, reordering, and re-presenting of meanings, practices, and subjectively experienced realities in a global context. In advanced capitalism, the modern culture of consumption reaches much further than ever before into the lives of people due to "changes in the social character of labor, in the social character of communications and in the social character of decision-making" (R. Williams 1977:125). These changes have affected migration processes. Expectations and new "visions of modern life and individual fulfillment that go with it" have motivated more people to migrate from more places in the world in the past two decades, including more people from Oaxacan communities (Portes and Rumbaut 1990:13; Pronk 1993; Salt 1989).

Although advanced capitalism is a major factor in contemporary patterns of migration, migration does not necessarily result from capitalist penetration (Hamilton and Chinchilla 1991:102–103). Global economic processes are filtered through nation-state policies. The state, as arbitrator of disparate interests, can maintain those structures that support the advanced capitalist enterprise, managing the contradictions and dislocations associated with its penetration and using migration as an escape valve. The state can assume a "gatekeeping" function, controlling the entrance of foreigners or the exit of its citizens (Hamilton and Chinchilla 1991:78). Or as in the case of Mexico, the Mexican state can do both simultaneously.

Mexican government officials are keenly aware that many rural areas are sustained not by agricultural activities, but by remittances of migratory income principally from the United States (Grindle 1988). The northward flow of immigrants creates tensions in the government's political relations with the United States. At the same time, however, Mexican political leaders are committed to neoliberal economic policies that support U.S. and Mexican corporate interests—policies that have consequentially increased the number of Mexican migrants entering the United States. Hence, the Mexican government finds itself in the paradoxical situation of sending its armed forces to guard the border in order to keep its citizens from crossing it while continuing to support policies that stimulate U.S.–bound migration. The undocumented Mexican migrants find themselves in the contradictory position of being desirable to a capitalistic country as a cheap source of labor yet spurned by the country's political system because they constitute a "silent invasion."

Crossing borders and at home, migrants have differential access to power. Marginalized peoples often internalize their own domination through commonsense notions that are the product of historical processes; these justifications make situations of inequality appear as "natural" outcomes of differences in racial or gendered intellectual capabilities (Gramsci 1971; B. Williams 1989). But people have questioned and renegotiated the racial, classist, and sexist hierarchies in which they have been situated, and they will continue to do so. Passive pawns they are not.[13] The concept of hegemony helps us to unite structure and agency and to understand how the social domination of one group over another is created and defended. As Raymond Williams (1977:112–114) discusses, hegemony is a process that must be re-created, modified, and defended against challenges from others who are outside or on the edge—those struggling for access to valued resources, for economic and symbolic capital.

Self-induction into the migrant labor process constitutes an important aspect of the regeneration of a migrant labor pool and the overall reproduction of the social order. Migrants reproduce themselves in the process of constituting themselves as political and social subjects, and in many cases, in an antagonistic relation to the prevailing structures. Migration studies need to recognize this contradictory nature and to comprehend how contradictions get played out in particular contexts. A key issue in this study is to understand how people, through their own activity and ideological development, contribute to the maintenance and reproduction of the social order and yet, at the same time, resist it.[14]

The processes of socioeconomic differentiation operate along many axes; the categories of gender, class, "race," nationality, and ethnicity are the most common terms used for hegemonic constructions of identity. These terms are historically charged.[15] Racial designations serve to deny cultural differences and essentialize social groups. They were assumed to be the result of "biological" differences among human groups. Ethnicity, on the other hand, represents how people construct their own identification in relation to the labor market. These identifications have changed through time, "as particular cohorts of workers gained access to different segments of the labor market and began to treat their access as a resource to be defended both socially and politically" (Wolf 1982:380).

Profits to the capitalist economy from the use of migrant labor depend on the construction of racist and xenophobic ideologies that legitimize the exploitation of their labor (Meillassoux 1981). The historical constructions of racial-class hierarchies are continually reenacted. However, many migrants (including many Putlecan migrants) empower themselves by actively maintaining several identities, connecting them to home and host nations. "By maintaining many different racial, national, and ethnic identities, transmigrants are able to express their resistance to the global political and economic situations that engulf them, even as they accommodate themselves to living conditions marked by vulnerability and insecurity. These migrants express this resistance in small, everyday ways that usually do not directly challenge or even recognize the basic premises of the systems that surround them and dictate the terms of their existence" (Glick, Basch, and Blanc-Szanton 1992:11).

Calagione (1992) and Rouse (1992) provide good examples of how this process is played out. In his study of Jamaican construction workers in New York City, Calagione shows that Jamaicans use recorded music and singing to "subtly control the pacing of the day's task, and to insert workers from different localities [in Jamaica] into the flow of the crew's work" (1992:22). By controlling time and the ethnic composition of the labor pool in the workplace, Jamaican immigrants are able to empower themselves in the face of exploitative labor hierarchies, yet their actions do not directly challenge the "system." Rouse demonstrates in his study of Mexicans in California how workers once in the United States do "internalize many of the values and beliefs associated with being good proletarian workers" but, at the same time, retain many of their convictions and meanings from their home community. The two views are often contradictory, causing tensions and confusion in the immigrants' daily lives, and result in what Rouse calls a "cultural bifocality, a capacity to see the world alternately through quite different kinds of lenses" (1992:41).

When women migrate, they have been traditionally assigned to the status of dependents (and their men to that of breadwinners) whether they have been working in remunerated activities in the receiving areas or not. This stereotype obscures and demeans women's active roles in all aspects of everyday life—as workers, mothers, educators, consumers, and so forth. By examining gender relations and the constructions of feminine/masculine subjectivities, we can see how gender roles and the organization of public and private life are rapidly changing and how migration directly impacts these transformations. Gender relations help determine the ways opportunities and limitations of broader political and economic forces are translated into different migration patterns (Hondagneu-Sotelo 1994). The construction of gender identities is intricately tied to work regimes, and migration can reinforce those constructions or illuminate some of their oppressive dimensions (Alonso 1992), which in turn can sometimes lead to an increase in women's self-esteem and independence.[16]

With the development of new multinational labor forces (i.e., the rapid incorporation of women of color into multinational export-processing industries and the expansion of service jobs) and the construction of racist and sexist ideologies used to recruit and to justify these labor forces, it becomes increasingly important to examine how axes of differentiation (gender, "race," age, class, nationality, ethnicity) are interwoven in both home and host societies and in relation to the state and the international economy, if we are to understand how hegemony is re-created and defended. As we enter the twenty-first century, we witness the growing and glaring disparity between "those who have" and "those who have not." Negotiating the ensuing contradictions in our everyday lives is a task we all share.

2

Negotiating Borders

The very idea of a map, with its implicit dependence upon the survey of a stable terrain, fixed referents and measurement, seems to contradict the palpable flux and fluidity of metropolitan life and cosmopolitan movement. Maps are full of references and indications, but they are not peopled. . . . With a map in our hands we can begin to grasp an outline, a shape, some sort of location. But that preliminary orientation hardly exhausts the reality in which we find ourselves.

(Chambers 1994:92)

*a*rriving in Putla to live for the second time, I could not believe how much the town had grown in two years: more people; more taco stands; and more dirt piles, stones, metal rods, and cement-mixing ponds to supply the numerous construction projects on what had been at my last visit vacant lots and agricultural lands. The map that I had of the town, which showed the community as a tightly bounded entity, certainly gave no hint of its physical growth, its changes. How does one begin to describe and understand change and migration to and from a community when peoples' lives continually spill over what a map demarks as its borders? The town called Putla occupies a particular terrain and its community members can tell you how to get there—its location—but even they cannot agree on where the town begins or ends.

During my second stay, I obtained a new map from the state tax office (figure 2.1). The map depicts geographically the place called Putla, yet a sense of fluidity emerges because of the town's roads' extending off in every direction, open and unending. Putla is linked to its closest neighbor without any divisional lines sharply separating the spaces. The map highlights the need to understand Putla's connections with other spaces and the people who occupy these spaces—friends, relatives, neighbors, business associates, government officials, and strangers.

Defining borders is a complex task, especially today as globalization accelerates at an unprecedented rate. We have entered a transnational age, one in which borders are more porous.[1] We cannot continue thinking about communities and nations or cultures and societies as

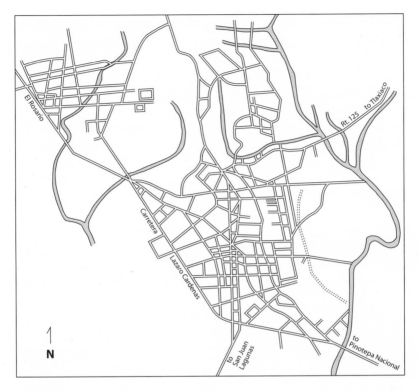

Figure 2.1. Putla de Guerrero, Oaxaca

"internally homogenous and externally distinctive," as "bounded objects" (Wolf 1982:6) Yet there is something that makes us feel that "who we are" is different from the identity of "those over there." And who we are, our self-conscious manipulation of identity, depends greatly on where we are. I remember the day a Putlecan working in a pizza shop in Atlantic City, New Jersey, gave my husband a free lemonade, calling him *paisano* (fellow countryman)—identifying with their common national roots in a foreign country. How different is this exchange from what occurred when we lived in provincial Mexico, where my husband is called "chilango" by the local people—marking their regional differences. Our identities are in part rooted in geography. Borders play an important role in distinguishing between "us" and "them." However, the lines are not fixed and closed, but flexible and fluid. The formation and the identification of who we are are grounded in space and in time.

There have always been inseparable connections between Putla and the Mixtec region in which it is situated and, to varying degrees at different historical moments, between Putla and larger cities (such as Tututepec, Tenochtitlán, Mexico City, Puebla, and Oaxaca City), the state of Oaxaca, the Mexican Republic, and other nations around the globe. The geographical fluidity of people for social, economic, or political reasons, on the one hand, disintegrates the notion of boundaries, yet on the other hand, people's sense of "self" includes identification with particular geographical spaces: it encompasses a sense of being Putlecan, Oaxacan, Mexican.

The state of Oaxaca is commonly described as a crumbled sheet of paper, which refers to its fragmented terrain of mountains and valleys. The state's fragmentation is also represented politically by its 570 municipalities, ethnically by the numerous indigenous groups, and linguistically by the sixteen distinct languages spoken by these ethnic groups. The town and district of Putla are located in the Mixtec region, an extensive and diverse area incorporating indigenous peoples (Mixtecs, Tacuates, Triquis, Amuzgos, Chochos) and people of mixed European, Native American, and African ancestries. The region extends from the western edge of the Valley of Oaxaca to the eastern side of Guerrero and from the Pacific Ocean to southern Puebla, and it is divided into three subregions: the Mixteca Baja, the Mixteca Alta, and the Mixteca de la Costa (figure 2.2).

The town of Putla is generally considered to be in the subregion of the Mixteca de la Costa and lies on its northern boundary (Dahlgren 1954:22–23; Romero Frizzi 1990:34; Spores 1967:7). More important than its location in the Mixteca de la Costa, however, is its location in the Valley of Putla, where the Mixteca Alta, the Mixteca Baja, and the Mixteca de la Costa join. Its position as a borderland has played a central role in its political and economic histories since pre-Hispanic times. The Valley of Putla served as a political boundary between warring pre-Hispanic states, between colonial royal magistrates and provinces, and between postindependence departments until the official creation of the district of Putla in the beginning of the twentieth century (Dahlgren 1954; Gerhard 1993:436; Spores 1967:14; Valdés 1993:15, 134).

Figure 2.2. Subdivisions of the Mixtec Region (Romero Frizzi 1990:35)
Reprinted with permission from INAH.

As a boundary between diverse ecological zones, the Valley of Putla has been, and is today, the site of an important regional marketplace that brings together people from towns throughout the Mixtec region and farther away. The pre-Hispanic and colonial north-south trade routes that crossed the western side of the Sierra Madre del Sur in Oaxaca ran through the Valley of Putla; the construction of the modern Mexican road number 125 followed these routes (Dahlgren 1954:239; Flanet 1977:28). Emphasizing Putla's commercial role, some Putlecans say that the name comes from *pochtecas,* the pre-Hispanic merchants who traveled great distances selling their goods.

Las Raíces [2]

Putla developed into a small kingdom (or city-state) sometime between A.D. 1000 and 1500. It was linked to other small kingdoms in the Mixtec region through a network of marriage and military alliances (Spores 1984:48). The site of one of the most important *ferias* in the Mixtec region during late pre-Hispanic times,[3] Putla marked the boundary between the kingdom of Tututepec and smaller kingdoms in the Mixteca Alta (Tlaxiaco, Achiutla, and Tilantongo).

The arrival of the Spanish in the first half of the sixteenth century marked a time of profound economic, political, religious, and social change for indigenous peoples. The introduction of Old World plants, animals, and technologies transformed productive activities. A new system of law and political order subordinated the indigenous population to the will of the Spaniards. Coercive efforts to convert indigenous peoples to the Spaniards' religious belief system led to the creation of new syncretic systems of religion to cope with Catholicism. Old World diseases ravaged indigenous populations. Putla and its neighboring communities experienced a dramatic reduction in population due to epidemics.[4]

The Spanish policy of indirect rule allowed indigenous communities to continue self-governing under the auspices of Spanish officials. Although the Crown proclaimed that its policies were to "protect" indigenous peoples from Spanish abuses, in practice they functioned to create and maintain economic and social boundaries. These boundaries were subjected to constant negotiation as indigenous peoples built syncretic economic systems based on their preexisting forms of organization and in response to imposed European tributary and mercantile economies (Greenberg n.d.). Colonial political regulations ensured Spanish domination in trade and extraction of labor and tribute from indigenous peoples, but at the same time indigenous groups worked to reclaim and defend their territories and ethnic identities (Carmagnani 1988).

The dialectic between communities' production/marketing and the colonial institutions shaped the content and pulse of economic and social activities with the result that the magnitude and scope of these activities in Putla and the Mixtec region varied through time and space. New productive activities, such as livestock and sugar production, arose and declined in accordance with the regional and global economic agendas as did the forms of tribute, such as cotton, cacao, and other agricultural products. Commerce became the principal economic activity of the Spanish in the Mixtec region, with new merchants and *alcaldes mayores*[5] gaining control over regional economics (Romero Frizzi 1990). Regional commercial activities did undergo profound changes, but the pre-Hispanic regional marketing system was not destroyed by the arrival of the Spanish. To the contrary, colonial trade reinforced the *tianguis*.[6] As the population in Putla slowly recuperated from the loss of lives caused by the epidemics, it regained its role as an important marketplace—the bridge between the mountainous regions and the coastal lowlands (Romero Frizzi 1990).

During the colonial period, a series of social hierarchies arose based on the intersections of class, "race," and gender differences. New economic activities led to new class relations; only now "race" colored those relations. Although pre-Hispanic society was stratified by class and by ethnic divisions, and the divisions between ethnic groups were often profound, social hierarchies were not based on "race." The homogenization of different indigenous ethnic groups as constituting one "Indian race" resulted from the processes of their subjugation by Spanish conquerors (Wolf 1982:380). The introduction of "race" as a category gave new form and meaning to discriminatory and subordinating practices. Unfortunately, these practices continue to plague the history of Putla, of the Mixtec region, and of Mexico from colonial times to today.

The racialized, violent masculinity of Spanish ruling practices demanded the labor of both indigenous women and men. Native women not only toiled with men in the mines, in the fields, and in sweatshops but were forced to provide sexual services. Sexual encounters between Spanish men and native women that resulted in the miscegenation of the population were often acts of rape.[7]

After the mid sixteenth century, women from Spain began arriving in the colony. Their economic and political power over native women encompassed a racialized moral dimension. White "purity" and "virtue" of the "superior" race, which set Spanish women apart from indigenous women, were embodied in the image of the Virgin Mary, the "civilized" Christian holy mother. The Catholic belief that all women should follow the Virgin Mary's divine example of humility, duty, and blind devotion, an assumption both Spanish men and women actively supported (men by policing women, women by living virtuously and by condemning native women's lifeways), made all women subservient to men. Adherence to the ideal models varied among women of different castes; not all women could afford to dedicate themselves solely to their husbands and children. Most had to work outside the home in order to survive (Lavrin 1985:42). Nevertheless, religious discourses and images helped enforce certain ruling practices, such as that men (like God) are to rule over women. The hierarchy of religious saints served to legitimize the social hierarchy as well.

Production for commodity exchange and a reliance on commodities transformed productive relations in New Spain. Colonized peoples became producers and consumers of commodities that served the colonizers' need for both raw materials and markets (Etienne and Leacock 1980). Key to the transformation was the ability of the colonial powers to control social and biological reproduction. Changing regulations governing marriage, inheritance, labor recruitment, and production resulted in conflicts among the colonizing agents—the Crown, the church, the conquistadors, and other colonists—in asserting control over women's reproduction of heirs and workers. Women experienced these changes differently, depending on their class position and ethnic identity. While European women were in short supply, indigenous women found opportunities to defend their collective interests. But as Spanish women arrived, the caste system and the patriarchal nuclear family emerged, supported by Crown and church rulings (Nash 1980:136–145).

Political and economic reforms following the founding of the new Republic of Mexico in the early nineteenth century produced a "series of transformations as massive in scale as any introduced by Spanish colonialism" (Greenberg 1989:185). Foremost was the granting to indigenous peoples of full citizenship and the discontinuation of apartheid-like legal institutions. New voting rights were supposed to increase democracy, but in practice native peoples did not gain more political power. In Oaxaca, one of the reforms that undermined indigenous autonomy was the reorganization of local government by *municipios* (counties). The switch from indirect to direct rule made native communities lose most of their local autonomy because it involved grouping them under a municipio, where *ladinos* (people of Spanish ancestry) dominated and served as agents of the state. New municipios formed in the Mixteca region included Putla, Juxtlahuaca, Huajuapan, and nine others (Pastor 1987:421).

By the mid nineteenth century, a series of national liberal reforms reduced the power of the church and the military, produced the country's first bill of rights, and prohibited corporate bodies from owning lands.[8] The aim of the last reform was to confiscate the massive landholdings of the Catholic Church in order to sell small parcels to indigenous people and mestizos. The idea was to make Mexico a country of small-scale landowners, but only rich Mexicans and foreign investors had money to buy land. Moreover, many indigenous communities lost their communal properties because these lands also fell under the new reform. The result was an even greater concentration of land in the hands of a few. Loss of lands and autonomy led many people in the Mixtec region, including a majority of Putlecans, to side with the French after they invaded Mexico in the 1860s (Berry 1981:88; Esparza 1988:275; Martínez 1883:324).

Land conflicts were complicated affairs, with the parties concerned using land titles and other documents from different eras to prove their claims. Beginning in the 1870s, the *cacique*[9] of Putla was involved in several land litigations with people in Putla's neighboring communities (La Laguna and El Rosario), with a doctor in Puebla, and later with several Triqui communities.[10] Several of the lands that Putla and El Rosario disputed were the same lands the doctor claimed, resulting in a litigation triangle (AGEO 1874, 1888, 1892, 1908).

Local disputes over land increased in the late nineteenth century as Porfirio Díaz's power and control grew and as European positivism became the prevailing doctrine in Mexico's political, philosophical, and social affairs. The commitment to laissez-faire development and foreign investments led to the "modernization" of industries and of communication and transportation systems at the cost of poverty and misery to the majority of the population. In Oaxaca, new factories produced beer, cigarettes, glass, and soap; a new railroad line connected Oaxaca to Puebla, via Tehuacán (Esparza 1988:278–279). But the poor got poorer. The effects of agricultural modernization were calamitous for peasant communities and for subsistence agriculture. Indigenous peoples and mestizos lost their lands, lived with rampant malnutrition and diseases, anguished under debt peonage, and were tyrannized by Díaz's *rurales* (national police force).

Díaz's policies advocated rapid industrialization financed by foreign capital and the expansion of the export economy. In Putla, the intensification of commercial crop production (tobacco and cotton) led to the reduction of lands used to grow basic food crops. National and foreign speculators seized lands to create new estates as the demand for raw materials by the cigar/cigarette and the textile industries expanded nationwide (Vallens 1978:35–42). By 1907, the production of tobacco equaled one-half million kilograms in the district of Putla, making Putla one of the largest tobacco-growing districts in Oaxaca (Esparza 1988:307). Sugarcane, on the other hand, did not increase in production in the region as it did elsewhere in the nation; *trapiches* (sugar mills) continued producing *panela* (unrefined sugar) and *aguardiente* (an alcoholic beverage) for local and regional markets (Rodríguez et al. 1989:173). The introduction of coffee, which resulted in a massive land grab by speculators in the coastal region of Oaxaca during this time, did not greatly impact the region of Putla until after the turn of the century (Greenberg 1989:188; Rodríguez et al.1989:176–180).

The Spencerian Darwinism dominant in Mexican positivism not only played a key role in justifying Díaz's economic policies but moreover fostered and elaborated racist ideas and attitudes born in colonialism. Evolutionary schemes fit each person into her or his "natural" niche. Díaz's circle of *científico* ("scientist") advisors believed in the "natural" inferiority of the indigenous population.[11] Immigration policies encouraged the entry of white foreigners and prohibited that of people of color in order to "whiten" the population (González 1970:154).

Científicos served the interests of themselves, of the creole upper class, and of foreign capitalism by promoting the financial enrichment of all three and by justifying the repression of the indigenous masses. However, other writings by social essayists, historians, educators, and romanticists during the Porfiriato (1876–1911, the period of Porfirio Díaz's presidency) challenged the racist ideology. Alternative viewpoints arose from liberal philosophies that asserted *mestizaje* (the fusion of two races) to be the essence of Mexican identity and the more advanced selection on the evolutionary scale because it combined the strengths of the two races. Some writers believed in the educability of the "Indian" and argued for a uniform, free, obligatory primary education system. They condemned the abject conditions in which indigenous peoples lived. Debates about the role positivists should play in indigenous communities extended throughout the duration of Díaz's reign (Stabb 1959).

Workers also challenged Díaz and the científicos. Workers' organizations in factories and mining grew and spread as the country industrialized. Radical newspapers helped forge thousands of laborers into mutualist and cooperativist organizations, and from these groups labor strikes were organized. The textile and cigar industries staged the largest number of strikes during the Díaz period. Mexican working-class women, who comprised the majority of workers in the rapidly expanding cigar/cigarette industry and a large part of the textile industry labor force, assumed active roles in the growing labor organizations and the strikes (Vallens 1978:51–59).

Women's lives underwent a dramatic shift in what was considered their "proper place" in society during the nineteenth century. Opportunities for women's education, which began under the Liberal administrations, grew during the late 1800s as many middle- and upper-class women battled with those positivists who sought to deny them access to education and to professional occupations. Working-class urban women, many of whom had migrated to the cities after having their agricultural lands expropriated or after escaping debt peonage, joined the ranks of factory workers. Supposed feminine qualities such as docility, submission to patriarchal authority, and willingness to work long hours for little pay made them particularly appealing to the factory owners, especially the owners of the textile and cigar factories (Vallens 1978:7–8). A hundred years later, the gendered rationale for using women as a cheap labor force in multinational export-processing industries in Mexico today echoes the one used in the late nineteenth century.

Transforming Borders

Since pre-Hispanic times, people living in the Putla region have actively adapted, negotiated, and resisted political, economic, and social changes. Indigenous lifeways were not eradicated by the initial Spanish conquest. To the contrary, indigenous groups continued to pursue their own cultural trajectories. As Carmagnani argues, the collapse of indigenous autonomy in Oaxaca was not a slow process but rather a drastic rupture during the mid nineteenth century as a result of the series of state and national liberal reforms initiated by the construction of the new nation-state (1988:229–238). However, even with the loss of autonomy, many ethnic identities have survived and ethnic groups continue to defend their lands and cultural practices.

As new processes impacted local, regional, state, and national arenas, boundaries and borders were transformed. The region of Putla has fluctuated in its position in the larger political and economic systems. In pre-Hispanic and colonial times, the region was an important center of production and commerce. Later, it became more marginalized in the state and national spheres with moments of greater integration, such as the tobacco years. Through the years, however, the town of Putla sustained its position as an important center of regional commerce, bridging the diverse ecosystems of the Mixtec region and, to varying degrees, connecting the region to national and international politics and economies—a role that continues to characterize Putla and Putlecans today.

•

3
Before the Road

I was always slow getting up before sunrise. Mother had to yell two or three times before I was awake. Grandmother would be grinding corn and mother making the fire. As the oldest, I had to help them with all the work. My favorite job was watching the fire. I used a *soplador* [palm fan], like this, to control how it burned. Too much air and the wood would burn too fast. Too little, it would die out. Mother and Grandmother made tortillas every day to sell in the market. Dad had some goats near Tierra Colorado and helped Grandfather in the *milpa* [cornfield] but he wasn't around all the time. Grandmother always said he couldn't stay put longer than three days. Sometimes he'd go to Silacayoapan, where my grandmother and aunt lived. He always brought me, my sister, and brother something special when he was gone a long time. One time he gave us new silk ribbons for our hair and my brother, his first leather belt. We were so excited . . . .

When I was thirteen, I'll never forget that morning when everything seemed strange. The sun had risen and as the light came in the open windows of our little house, I could see my uncle and two oldest cousins talking to Grandfather. We only had two rooms then, dirt floors and a few chairs and a table that Grandfather had made. I was in the kitchen with Mother and Grandmother, who were working in silence. Mom looked worried. Suddenly they [uncle and cousins] grabbed their shotguns and jumped on their horses. Dust flew everywhere as they rode out of town fast. Mother started yelling at Pedro to fetch some water.[1] Pedro has always been a bit *distraído* [absentminded], but Mother never spoke so harshly to him as she did that morning. He shuffled down the dirt path to the river. I slowly rolled up the *petates* [palm mats] except for the one on which Gaby [her younger sister] played. Grandfather sat in the hammock motionless with his head cupped in his hands. He had killed two iguanas yesterday for tamales and they sat unskinned. Finally Grandmother motioned him to come have a cup of hot chocolate and some *pan de yema* [bread made with egg yolk] that Aunt Lupita had left over from yesterday. Uncle Francisco used to bake wonderful bread, which Aunt Lupita sold in the market alongside my mom under the biggest mango tree. She always gave us some bread when we passed by there on the way home from school. Anyway, I later discovered that it was on this day my mother and grandparents learned of my father's shooting. By the time my uncle and cousins got to Chilapa, my father was dead. He had gotten into a fight in a cantina [bar] and was shot. They couldn't even get his body because no one knew where he was buried or, at least, that's what they said. My mother's heart became sad and even though she was only thirty-four, she was never with another man. She always told us that when you marry it's until you die. We've never had any divorces in our family, and everyone has been married in the church. I think that's why people respect us. My mother set a good example. She worked hard to raise us. . . .

Putla was a much smaller town before the road. Everybody knew everybody and you could count on friends and family to help when you needed it. We didn't have much but it didn't seem to matter. At night we often listened to stories my grandfather would tell about the spirits and ghosts who roam around here or stories about the revolution, which Pedro loved. Grandfather was only a boy then, but he always managed to put himself in the middle of any battle. My grandmother didn't like him to tell these stories. She said it was bad for children to hear such things. After my father died, he never told another bloody story.

(Putlecan woman, sixty-two years old)

*i*n 1950, fewer than 3,000 people lived in the town of Putla (INEGI 1950). Older Putlecans recount how the town's cobblestone and dirt streets were lined with simple wood and adobe homes. A few larger, more elegant houses and the town's public office stood in the middle of the community around the kiosk. There were no public water or drainage systems. Some Putlecans had wells in their backyards, but most had to carry water in metal buckets or clay jars to their homes from a river or a neighbor's well. Kerosene lamps and a few electric lights powered by a privately owned generator in the Hacienda de la Concepción provided Putlecans with several hours of light at night.[2] Few people stayed up late, however, because most earned a living from subsistence farming and rose at daybreak to start work.

Health in the town and region seemed to be improving when a national vaccination program put an end to smallpox epidemics. Malaria continued to kill more than 6,000 people a year in the tropical lowlands of Oaxaca, but overall life expectancy improved and the infant mortality rate dropped throughout the region (Ornelas 1988:137–138). Although health improvements suggest a heightened standard of living, life in the countryside continued to be characterized by grinding poverty as well as lower life expectancies and higher rates of infant mortality than in urban centers.

The Mexican state had begun increasing its influence and control throughout the nation since the Mexican Revolution at the beginning of the century. The Constitution of 1917 marked an end to Díaz's laissez-faire modernization with reforms in land tenure, labor rights, education, and women's rights. A new kind of revolutionary nationalism emerged, redefined "the Mexican national culture as a mestizo culture," and "provided the ideological platform for a protectionist economy and a strong state" (Lomnitz-Adler 1992:9).

Due to the gap between what appeared legally on paper and what changes were put into practice, there is much debate over how little or how much life changed after the revolution. Women, for example, gained the right to divorce, to equal authority in the family, and to work outside the home, but the new 1917 law was at odds with social reality (Leahy 1986:47–64). "The stigma of illegitimacy and the real barriers to women's access to higher-level professions and business opportunities remained" (Nash 1980:145). In Putla, wealthier women's desires to study medicine, law, or business when they were young were crushed by fathers who saw no need for their daughters to study a profession. Older Putlecan women recount how their fathers believed that it would be a waste of time and money because their daughters were to marry, have children, and tend to the affairs of the home.

Postrevolutionary reforms in land tenure and in education had little impact on the people in the district of Putla until the 1930s. Between 1920 and 1923, the number of solicitations for land in the district of Putla outnumbered those of all other Oaxacan districts; twenty-two groups petitioned the agrarian commission in Oaxaca City for agricultural lands in the Putla district. Not one was granted. Thirty-nine percent of the state's total 133 petitions came from the Mixtec region—more than from any other region in the state. Then-president Obregón returned lands to only eleven groups in the state, one of which was in the Mixtec region (Ruiz 1988:408–411).

Agriculture remained the basis of the local economy in Putla as elsewhere in the state of Oaxaca. The production of basic food crops (corn, beans, chiles, and wheat) and export crops (coffee, tobacco, sugar, and bananas) continued to comprise the greatest volume of agricultural products in the decades following the revolution (Arellanes 1988:75). The steady increase of land allotment for the production of coffee in the early twentieth century obstructed peasants in their petitions for the restoration of lands. In 1932, only six of twenty-nine petitions from Putla met with a favorable response, because of the national policy of "respecting" coffee estates (Arellanes 1988:122–124).

During the presidency of Lázaro Cárdenas (1934–1940), the national government became responsive to agrarian issues and to the rights of native peoples. The number of hectares redistributed in Oaxaca increased four times from the amount returned in the period between 1916 and 1934. In the earlier period, half of the hectares allotted were located in the state's central valleys. Under Cárdenas, 70 percent of the lands were restored to people in the districts of Jamiltepec, Juchitán, Tuxtepec, and Putla. Between 1916 and 1940, restoration of 3,602 hectares of land in the district of Putla included 993 hectares of rain-fed agricultural lands, 2,600 hectares of forested lands, and 10 hectares of irrigated lands (Ornelas 1988:144–147). After decades of fighting, the communities located around the sugar estate of La Concepción had their lands restored. The plantation workers formed an *ejido*,[3] and they changed the name of the community to La Concepción del Progreso (AGN 1936). But for many indigenous groups, land conflicts continued. In 1937 the Triquis of San Miguel Copala began protesting against the invasion of their communal lands by landowners from Putla and El Rosario (AGN 1937). Their protests continue to this day and the disputed area includes lands that constitute half of the present-day town of Putla. Other Triqui groups from Llano de Nopal and from La Luz Copala have also been fighting with landowners from Putla and El Rosario since the mid twentieth century (García 1973:176–180, 198).

The corporatist model of rule institutionalized in the 1930s allowed the conservative regimes of the 1940s and the 1950s to adjust agrarian reform laws under the guise of "modernization." New amendments gave protection to wealthier landowners via the courts. Investments in agriculture including the large irrigation projects were concentrated in the northern region of the country. Subsidies to modernized farmers and price controls for the major food crops left undercapitalized peasant producers vulnerable and unable to meet their needs. In order to curb peasant unrest, the succeeding Mexican presidents, each from the Partido Revolucionario Institucional (PRI), continued to dispense marginal lands or "paper rights to land that would require years of bureaucratic struggle for realization" (Foley 1995:62). Between 1940 and 1964, Mexican presidents granted fewer than 95,000 hectares of rain-fed lands and forestlands to people in the district of Putla (Segura 1988:243)—a symbolic gesture that in no way addressed the needs of peasant farmers. Wealthier Putlecans maintained ownership of the most productive lands.

The economic and social conditions of agricultural production in Putla and throughout the state made peasant farmers vulnerable. "A drought, a bad harvest, a plague, an unexpected accident or sickness, an onerous *cargo*,[4] or death" forced families to find work elsewhere in order to earn the extra revenue needed for daily survival (Ornelas 1988:181). Temporary migration to work on commercial crop plantations became the option increasingly used by peasant farmers. With the population multiplying and access to land limited, more and more peasants were forced to migrate seasonally to work on plantations as day laborers. Many members of poorer families from Putla migrated to coffee plantations in Chiapas and in coastal Oaxaca.

When the U.S. government initiated the Bracero Program (a guest worker program for Mexicans in the United States; *bracero* literally means "day laborer") in the 1940s and sent recruiters to Oaxaca, men from Putla jumped at the opportunity to work in the United States, believing that they would be able to increase their incomes sufficiently to invest in a small enterprise, such as cultivating coffee plants, when they returned home. Some did manage to save enough to build a home, but most had their illusions crushed by the hard work and the meager salaries paid. For many Putlecans, seasonal migration to the U.S. Southwest at harvest time became a way of life and continued after the Bracero Program ended in 1964.

In the 1950s, coffee became the most important export crop in the state of Oaxaca, with production increasing by 50 percent over the previous decade's rate (Segura 1988:209). Coffee replaced tobacco as the principal cash crop grown in the district of Putla. With coffee prices on the international market reaching an all-time high, families planted small coffee orchards on lands previously used for subsistence crops. By 1970, coffee production in the district comprised 10 percent of the state's and 1 percent of national production (García Alcaraz 1973:47). Coffee producers saw little of the profit, however. Lacking the means to transport their product, producers had to sell to coffee buyers from Tlaxiaco, Juxtlahuaca, and Putla.

Coffee production tied the community to the international market but only through a group of intermediaries. Producers sold their coffee beans to local buyers, who established and maintained business relations in several cities. By the late 1950s, three sons of a Spanish merchant in Putla outcompeted the other coffee buyers and monopolized the buying.[5] One of the sons, estranged from his brothers, later bought modern equipment to process the coffee beans in order to export coffee directly to the United States (García Alcaraz 1973:93). Owning the largest general store in Putla, he has extended credit for goods and loans to farmers at high interest rates and has become wealthier by the same strategy used by many coffee buyers in the state: buying cheap and selling high (Greenberg 1989:193).

Commerce remained the focal point of the local economy. People came from rural communities throughout the region to sell or exchange locally produced foods and goods in the weekly tianguis. Vendors laid their products on blankets in the open-air market under the shade of large mango trees. Agricultural products comprised the bulk of commodities sold, accompanied by a modest range of regional commercial goods, such as petates; baskets; *metates* (grinding stones); and ceramic jars, bowls, and *comales* (flat dishes used to cook tortillas). Pottery from the Mixteca Alta was traded in Putla for peppers, fish, and other lowland products (Ravicz 1965:75). Imported merchandise (e.g., hardware, leather saddles, refined sugar, candles, and manufactured cloth and clothing) was found only in the larger general stores, owned by the wealthier merchant-landowning families.

Consumption patterns had changed little since the turn of the century. Most Putlecans wore manufactured clothing or clothes they made from store-bought fabrics, but few owned shoes other than huaraches (leather sandals). Corn, beans, chiles, and fruits formed the basis of the diet and were supplemented with milk, breads, sweetened coffee, and hot chocolate, and sometimes domestic and wild meats. Some people boast that the best *arroz con leche* (rice pudding) was made in Putla with fresh milk from El Rosario, sugar from Concepción del Progreso, rice from the Hacienda de Guadalupe, and wild vanilla from the Cerro de la Campana. Sugarcane grown throughout the district continued to be processed into panela and aguardiente. García Alcaraz (1973:103) notes in his research on Triqui communities that a large part of their sparse revenue earned from coffee was spent on aguardiente.

Times were slowly changing, however. Before the late 1940s, goods were carried in and out of the town on the backs of mules, horses, and people. Increasing communication and transportation in Oaxaca bypassed most of the Mixtec region during the first half of this century. The region was to be traversed by a railroad line that would run from Puebla to the Chacahua lagoon on Oaxaca's Pacific coast, but the project was abandoned due to legal problems and to new studies in 1936 and 1938 that refuted the profitability of the carbon and coal resources in the region (Ornelas 1988:140). In the 1940s, the arrival of biplanes made commutes between Putla and Acapulco, Mexico City, and other regional towns faster and easier, but only a minority could afford this convenience. Biplanes began bringing more external goods to the region, such as steel machetes made in Monterrey (Tibón [1961] 1984:175). But as a Putlecan pointed out in an interview in the late 1950s, increased accessibility to the region at this time did not modify the way most Putlecans thought or lived because for the most part only the wealthy traveled and used this service. "Putla, aislado e incomunicado hasta hace poco, se alcanza ahora en setenta minutos de vuelo. Un brinco de sólo 280 kilómetros desde la capital; pero, en el tiempo, la distancia es de dos siglos. Putla es una muestra viviente del México del siglo XVIII . . . . Sólo que ahora los gachupines y los criollos forman un bloque compacto con los mestizos para explotar a los indios"[6] (Ricardo Martell; cited in Tibón [1961] 1984:157). The construction of a network of roads in the 1950s in Oaxaca integrated regions, and commerce expanded as transport became easier. Air service declined after the completion of the road from Putla to the Mexico City–Oaxaca City highway in the late 1950s. Vehicle transport spurred the greater flow of goods and people in and out of the district.[7]

The Putlecan Elite

Putla was not only a commercial center for the region but was also the seat of political and economic power and control. Following the revolution, Putla, like the rest of Oaxaca, was "left primarily to tend to its own affairs" (Murphy and Stepick 1991:43). The local elite maintained their position despite the few successful attempts to redistribute their lands. The perspective of the elite can be seen in the following account:

> My father owned a lot of land—all cattle ranches around Mesones, Las Huertas, Putla, and El Rosario. He bought calves and sold them grown in the Mixteca Alta. We lived here in Putla but would ride to the other ranches on horseback with big palm leaves held above my sister and my heads to give us shade. My sister and I would bathe in milk to keep our skin pure. On the ranches, we used to play with *mozos* [boys] whose parents worked for our father until we got a little older and it wasn't proper. We would watch them drink milk out of leaves and eat with their hands. . . .
>
> Mom died when I was six, so Dad sent us to live with our grandmother in Mesones but we hated it, so he sent us to a convent in Oaxaca for a proper education. He loved to read and he always bought us lots of books. I wanted to be a doctor but he told me, "only men are doctors," so I learned to sew. I started the sewing school here thirty years ago, and I still love to teach. It helped, too, when times got bad. Many years ago, my father's trapiche was stolen from him. He worked hard every day, sunrise to sunset, and then suddenly the government said he had to give some of his lands to those *indios* [indigenous people]. What a terrible day. You know, Cárdenas was not the great president that everyone says he was.
>
> (Putlecan woman, early sixties)

In the town of Putla, Spaniards and the descendants of Spaniards, of Italians, and of British comprised the core of the local Putlecan elite. They owned large haciendas throughout the region but lived primarily in their townhouses in Putla next door to or above their general stores. A strict separation of classes was maintained not only economically but also politically and socially. The local elite men controlled the town's presidency. Conflict and fighting pervaded local elections as wealthy families vied for control. Sons and daughters followed their parents' exogamous marriage customs, many seeking mates while in private schools in Mexico City, Puebla, or Oaxaca City.

Elite families participated in community festivals and service activities. When they had to perform *tequio* service,[8] they completed their community obligations by hiring other Putlecans to do the work in their names. They often served as *mayordomos* (festival sponsors) of religious celebrations, but they never intermingled with nonelite community members in private social occasions. A daughter of one of the wealthiest families recalled the first "mixed" dance (one in which all community members were invited regardless of class) in 1965. She desperately wanted to attend, but her father refused to let her. "I don't think any of the [elite] parents allowed their children to go. Maybe a few secretly went. It was a big thing for the town" (Putlecan woman, late fifties).

Although the elite class rarely interacted socially with the rest of the mestizo population, the two groups did share the racist belief that they were superior to the indigenous peoples in the region. Few indigenous people actually lived in the town of Putla, but many, especially Triquis from neighboring communities, worked on Putlecan ranches and in their agricultural fields as day laborers and in their houses as servants. Putlecans did not bother to learn Triqui names, instead calling the men "Tatani" or "José" and the women "María." Parents and children of all classes addressed Triqui adults with the informal *tú* (you) (Tibón 1984:164). "Sobresale, en Putla, nuestro lamentable complejo de superioridad sobre el indio. . . . No sólo los mestizos acomodados, sino también los pobres"[9] (Ricardo Martell; cited in Tibón [1961] 1984:164).

Indigenous people, on the other hand, addressed mestizos and ladinos with respectful titles: *el señor, la señora,* or *la señorita.* They stepped to the side of the street or path and cast their faces toward the ground whenever a Putlecan passed by. Few Triquis challenged the local elite, even though they were routinely exploited by these merchants in commercial transactions (García Alcaraz 1973:31, 99). Protests over encroaching Putlecan landowners have been ignored by local officials. The Triquis did not hesitate, however, to kill animals owned by non-Triquis who grazed on their communal lands, and Putlecans rarely entered their communities for fear of their lives. Putlecans believed the Triquis to be *salvajes* (wild, savages) because the Triquis had scant material goods and were illiterate and monolingual.[10]

State Education and Family Life

One of the goals of the postrevolution government was to provide primary education for all citizens. Through education, the national government gained more control over the population. By making school programs and rural teachers dominant in everyday activities, they diminished the influence of the Catholic Church. It was hoped that indigenous peoples would "modernize" and assimilate into a pan-Mexican culture. The incorporation of *indigenismo* into the official orthodoxy of the new regime was part of the nation-building process. Whereas Díaz had tried to integrate indigenous peoples into the nation-state by brute force and by eradicating their lifeways, the postrevolutionary government believed that they could be integrated without de-Indianization. "Integration would be planned, enlightened and respectful of that [Indian] culture" (Knight 1990:80).

Paradoxically, indigenismo was imposed on indigenous people from the outside and was an elite project that in no way addressed issues of real concern to native groups, such as agrarianism, which had popular roots. The building of a strong Mexican nation resided in its "mestization," according to the influential José Vasconcelos, minister of education from 1921 to 1924 and paladin of the "cosmic race." Both mestizos and indigenous peoples would contribute to creating a hybrid culture of which the whole would be greater than its two parts (Knight 1990). Mestizaje was equated with nationhood.

Even though the romanticized version of the "Indian" was revered and praised in artistic and literary circles in Mexico and though the indigenismo-mestizaje doctrines formed a central part of the official state ideology, racist ideologies permeated and placed blame on living indigenous peoples for obstructing progress and national development. "Indianness" was, and continues to be, equated with inferiority and with the lack of material goods and of social competence. Although native languages are officially endorsed, their use is unofficially discouraged (Knight 1990).

The first public primary school opened in Putla in 1936. Most poorer Putlecans were illiterate, as illustrated by the 98 percent illiteracy rate of the members of twenty-four campesino organizations in the district of Putla in 1934 (Arellanes 1988:67). Previously, only wealthier Putlecans had the resources to educate their families in Catholic schools in Puebla, Mexico City, and Oaxaca City. By 1950, almost half of the Putlecan population was literate. Most children started elementary school, but often they only attended one or two years.

Many Putlecan parents believed their children had enough education once they could write their names and the alphabet and had acquired some basic reading and arithmetic skills. Their labor was needed to help support the family. Boys followed their fathers and grandfathers to work in the fields or care for the livestock. Girls helped their mothers wash clothes in the river, shell and grind corn to make tortillas or tamales, and care for the animals in the backyard. They often accompanied their mothers to the market to sell homemade foods or produce their families had harvested. Parents held absolute authority over their children. "We always obeyed our parents and grandparents, did what we were told to do. When visitors came to the house, we were not allowed to talk. When my brother was little, he once got mad at our cousin and began yelling at him in the house where our parents were talking. My father took him outside and whipped him—he couldn't sit down for the rest of the day. It was different back then" (Putlecan woman, mid-sixties).

Patriarchal authority along with age determined the social hierarchies of the family. Family honor depended on women's virtue and men's ability to protect the women's reputations. Putlecan women spent most of their time with other women, especially their *compadres* and other female relatives.[11] Rarely was a woman in the company of a man who was not a relative. Young women were always chaperoned when a young man came to visit or when the young couple went to a dance or any other social event.

Most Putlecan women never traveled beyond the boundary of the region. The rationale of needing to protect female family members prohibited women from accompanying their husbands on their migratory journeys, even though, many older Putlecan women recounted to me, they begged their husbands to let them go with them. Husbands replied that the journeys were too dangerous and that wives were better off at home where male relatives could look after them.

At the center of the family, Putlecan women were in charge of teaching morals and values to the children. Their actions were scrutinized by community members. Any "improprieties" a woman or her children committed became fuel for community gossip and often led to violence. Men adhering to ideas of machismo (manliness) felt obliged to defend the honor of their families "with a gun, if necessary." Men were not subjected to the same standards set for women. They were expected to have illicit relationships because of their "hot blood." Sexual prowess was an important element in the defining of a man's manliness. In the region of Putla, the practice of having lovers who bore illegitimate children was widespread and caused disputes, often bloody, over inheritance rights once the fathers died. Sometimes properties were distributed among both legitimate and bastard children.

> My father had many lovers. That's why my mother took my brother and left to live in D.F. [Federal District] She couldn't stand to see them pregnant. I lived with my aunt and father here in the big house and worked in his four stores. . . . After he died, everyone started fighting. People I didn't even know came to claim part of his lands and money. I didn't fight, so all I got was this house and some land near La Laguna. I should have inherited everything since I'm his only legitimate child in Putla. But the law isn't the law, you know, not now, not then. Now I wished I had fought for it. Not for me, but for my children.
>
> (Putlecan woman, late fifties)

Even with conflicts and turmoil, the family was, and continues to be, the fundamental social unit in Putla as elsewhere in Mexico. One's identity in the community was to a large extent defined by one's family.

Changes to Come

Before the construction of the road that linked Putla to the larger road network, the rhythm of daily life in the community was essentially rural.

People rose with the sun and went to bed soon after it set. The agricultural cycle defined the passing of the year. Economic activities centered on crop production, animal husbandry, and limited commerce with agrarian communities throughout the region. As peasant-vendors, the Putlecans' sources for cash were minimal. Wealth was concentrated in the hands of the local elite.

As the small town's population slowly grew, more and more Putlecans found themselves without land or unable to produce enough to support their families by subsistence farming. For many, the solution was to migrate. Many joined the multitude of rural citizens who made their way to a big city, especially to Mexico City. Others continued to work as *braceros* in the United States or on export-crop plantations in Oaxaca and neighboring states part of the year and then return home to Putla to tend to their crops the rest of the time. Migration supplemented families' earnings but still remained of minor importance in the local economy. Once the road was completed in 1960, however, changes in Putlecan lifeways were to occur with increasing speed.

4
After the Road

Some of the best people of our time speak now only in this dark language. Their grave voices have to compete with the jingle of happy consumption, the only widespread form of contemporary optimism.

(R. Williams 1985:21)

*O*n a Sunday morning during Mass, the local priest in Putla implores the members of his congregation to take care of the land that God entrusted to them. Two banners hang down on each side of the pulpit painted with vibrant tropical scenery and the words *protect* and *preserve* in bold letters across the bottom. After a half hour of reprimanding the members of the congregation for their flagrant disregard of "God's gift" and for their indiscriminate consumerism, the priest wipes the sweat from his brow and, breathless, gives the benediction. The people shuffle out the church doors, anxious to get on with the most important business of the day—marketing.

Sunday is the main market day in Putla. The streets are lined on both sides with people selling their goods: dried fish and shrimp from the coast; chiles, tomatoes, and cilantro from the Copalas (San Miguel Copala, La Luz Copala, and other Triqui areas in the lower elevations); plastic containers, chairs, and metal cookware from Puebla and the Federal District; bushels of apples from the Tarahumara region in Chihuahua. People pour into the town to join the local residents in their weekly bargaining. Some vendors come as early as Friday evening to find a good spot to set up shop on the town's newly paved streets. By Sunday evening as the last pickup trucks overloaded with people head out of town, the streets become quiet. Discarded potato chip bags, ice-cream wrappers, plastic soda bags and straws, rotted vegetables, fruit skins, and other refuse from the merchants' booths are the reminders of the day's busy activities. Content with their sales but grumbling about the mess, the townspeople complain about the authorities and their inability to do something about the trash that covers the streets.

When I returned to Putla in 1993 after a two-year absence, I was shocked and dismayed by how much trash had accumulated in and around the town. I discovered, however, that a local ecology group, La Agrupación Ecologista Lugar de Neblina, had formed in the beginning of the year to find a solution to the growing pollution problem. By the time I arrived, the group was busy spreading their message of reducing consumption and of recycling containers in order to clean up the town. The priest had donated the use of the church courtyard as a temporary recycling collection center. Seeing the small piles of glass, cardboard, and metal ready for transport to a recycling center in Puebla made me enthusiastic about the group's plan of action. I became more so while conducting a survey for my own research and inadvertently gathered information that I thought supported the goals of the Agrupación.

One of the questions I asked residents was to describe the things they liked and disliked about their town. Although I expected a wide assortment of answers, people repeatedly stated that they liked the natural beauty of Putla's countryside and its rivers and that they disliked the trash, which was thrown everywhere and was destroying the area's harmony. Of the families I surveyed, a quarter ranked ecological problems as their primary concern. More than half listed trash, *aguas negras* (waters contaminated with sewage), and the cutting of forests as three of the town's biggest problems. I believed that if the people were genuinely concerned about the pollution problem, then the Agrupación should have been able to get the townspeople rallied behind its ideas and solutions. But it never happened. Only a few people came to the meetings. Not only did many of the townspeople fail to support the Agrupación, but some even belittled the group's efforts. My curiosity about the contradiction between people's beliefs and desires and their actions led me to examine how and why people would increase consumption in a time of economic crisis; why they would resist a campaign that supported their desire for a cleaner Putla; and what, if any, was the role of migration in these paradoxes.

Increasing Integration into the Nation-State and the Global Economy

In the late 1950s, after the completion of the paved road from Putla north to the Mexico City–Oaxaca City highway and south to Pinotepa Nacional, movement of goods and people in and out of the region increased as trucks, buses, and cars began replacing the costlier air service and the slower pedestrian and equestrian forms of transport. Trucks carrying nationally manufactured goods began inundating the town. Many of the cheaper products eventually outcompeted locally produced goods. Factory-made sodas put an end to the local, family-run *gaseosas* (carbonated fruit drinks) business. Prepackaged foods filled store shelves, along with bundles of synthetic cloth, factory-made clothing, and plastic shoes. Mattresses replaced palm mats. Hand-made tortillas, which took hours to prepare, were replaced by tortillas that came out of a machine on a conveyor belt in minutes. The promotion of metal pots, glass dishes, and plastic containers as more durable and more sanitary reduced pottery sales. Homes made of concrete and steel rods began to replace those made of adobe and tile. Promises of increased harvests with the use of new chemical fertilizers and pesticides drew farmers to the credit lines, especially farmers investing in coffee plants. As older Putlecans often told me, "After the road, everything changed."

Public works initiated in the town in the 1960s included installation of electrical power, piping of water from the rivers to private holding tanks, and construction of a small hospital. In the 1970s, a drainage system was laid to carry sewage from the town underground to the river. New telephone lines expanded service to private homes. As vehicle transport grew, mechanic shops and tire service stores emerged while sales of leather saddles, bits, and other horse supplies withered. Car and truck owners began demanding better roads; concrete pavement started to replace the old cobblestone and dirt streets.

Putla serves as the cabecera (the political-administrative center) of the district as well as the link with Mexican national society. It is the center of regional commerce and public services. The town now has dozens of permanent specialized stores covering a wide spectrum of products, including hardware, clothes, shoes, toys, furniture and appliances, groceries, stationery, agricultural supplies, music and videos, and so on, unlike the smaller villages in the district, which typically have only one or two small general stores. Putla is the district's center for education, with schooling beyond the elementary level: two junior high schools, one high school (COBAO), a teachers college (Escuela Normal), and an adult education program. Judges; police; doctors; dentists; veterinarians; tax officials; electricity, telephone, and postal services; and registrars for marriage, birth, and death certifi-

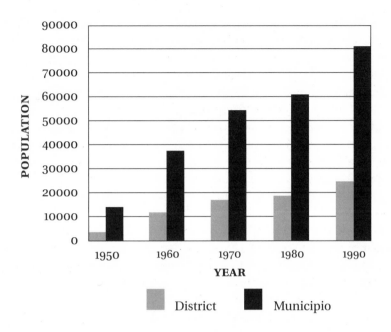

Figure 4.1. Population of the Municipality and District of Putla, 1950–1990 (INEGI 1950, 1963, 1972, 1984, 1992)

cates and for property deeds are concentrated in Putla, connecting the people of the local district with the state and the nation.

Public services have unsuccessfully struggled to keep pace with the needs of the growing population. The district's population has doubled in the last three decades. The municipio of Putla has had the highest growth rate in the district, culminating in a population of approximately 25,000 people by 1990 (figure 4.1).

The dramatic increase in population is due to higher birth and lower infant mortality rates within the community and to in-migration from the surrounding region, especially from the Mixteca Alta.[1] Ecological deterioration of agricultural lands, lack of access to water, increasing landlessness, shortages of firewood and other communal forest resources, and under- and unemployment in the region have forced families, no longer able to support themselves with subsistence and semisubsistence farming alone, to seek alternative ways to support themselves. The agrarian crisis became more acute in many districts in the state, including Putla, when the world price for coffee plummeted in the 1980s, compelling families to abandon their coffee orchards.

The solution for many families in the Mixtec region was to send members to other areas for work. Many Triqui families began their annual migration to Sinaloa or to Sonora to work in commercial agriculture harvests. Other people in the region left to find work in the cities or in the United States. Some husbands who did not want to be so far from their families and their lands came to the "city" of Putla. Compared to their hometowns, Putla seemed to be a bustling urban center.

Finding work in construction and in other daily-wage jobs in Putla, some men began setting up makeshift homes on the edges of town and were soon joined by some members of their families while other members stayed in their hometowns to continue tending the fields. Alternating between their hometowns and Putla became possible as a result of the increase in the number of pickup trucks, which now provide relatively quick and inexpensive transportation in the region.[2] Land invasions, under-the-table deals with local politicians who sold sections of land belonging to the town, and the division of croplands into minuscule lots made land accessible to newcomers—land on which they built small homes piece by piece. Building in these new housing areas quickly outpaced the provision of water and drainage services, and many lots still lack street access.

The rapid growth of the town has caused not only infrastructural problems but also divisions among the townspeople. Even though many families living in Putla today are descendants of Mixtecs and mestizos from communities outside the district who moved to Putla in the late nineteenth and early twentieth centuries,[3] people mark the completion of the paved road as the dividing line between those who are "authentic" Putlecans (preroad) and those who are "outsiders" (postroad). "Before the road, the town was tranquil. Everybody knew everyone else. If a stranger arrived in town, the town president would find out why he was here. Now we have violence, murders, and drugs—all brought here by the ignorant people from the countryside" (Putlecan man, fifty-four years old).

Framed as unscrupulous and as *gente sin razón* (uncivilized people) by "authentic" Putlecans, "outsiders" posed a threat to one's lands and to the overall safety of the town. In the 1980s, "outsiders" invaded the section of Putla where the airstrip and the cemetery were located and formed an ejido. The owner of the land, who lived in Oaxaca City, failed to prove that the land was in use because air service had ended long ago and the land stood empty. Wood shacks now cover the hill from the road up to the flat airstrip. Many townspeople scorn the members of the ejido, saying that these "outsiders" stole the land. They fear that no land is safe.

"Outsiders" are blamed for bringing drugs into the community, for gunfire at night, and for murders. Male day laborers from the region who sleep in the town plaza and who are seen drinking in public at night reinforce these ideas that are applied uniformly to all "outsiders"—even though most come to find work to support their families and maybe to earn enough to send some of their children to junior high school. Moreover, although conflicts, shootings, and theft occurred frequently in the town before the new road, people forget that part of the town's history when discussing the new arrivals, thus creating a romanticized version of their past.

At Home and in the Republic

For many people from villages in the region, the town of Putla is viewed as providing numerous opportunities, even though the entire region is one of the poorest in Mexico. While husbands work as day laborers, wives sell sandwiches, popcorn, flavored waters, and other homemade foods on the street to supplement their spouses' paltry earnings. Other women wash clothes or work in the string of new taco stands along the main road. "There's plenty of work and money in this town. Everything sells here," women told me repeatedly. Compared to the dire situations in their hometowns, Putla is a place of hope. As one woman commented, "We are poor but at least we can eat well here. At home we only ate a few tortillas with a little chile."

The perspective that "outsiders" hold of Putla as a place of opportunity is quite different from the views espoused by the "authentic" Putlecans, especially since the 1982 economic crisis swept across the nation. In 1982, when the world price for oil dropped and Mexican capital flowed out of the country, the de la Madrid administration accepted the conditions and structural adjustment criteria required by the IMF and the World Bank "for a minimally sufficient infusion of credit" (Goldrich and Carruthers 1992:100). Economic neoliberalism became orthodoxy, resulting in a substantial reduction in social welfare spending. The structural adjustment program's impact on the standard of living for all Mexicans was severe. Real income, social services, and material resources declined. In the countryside, the average daily wage dropped 40 percent (Calva 1988:76). Decreases in guaranteed prices for basic crops further impoverished farmers. Foreign investments in agriculture went to commercial export growers, making subsistence farmers even more marginalized. As Goldrich and Carruthers summarize, "Just at the point where Mexico needed stronger support than ever before for environmental protection and sustainable development, structural adjustment undercut both" (1992:102).

Agricultural production in the region fell to an all-time low in the 1980s, forcing families to develop new strategies to survive. The inability of agricultural production to support families caused sons and daughters of farmers to search for alternative occupations. In my survey in the town of Putla, over half of the parents worked in agriculture whereas only 5 percent of their children did. Many children had left to make a new life in a larger city or in the United States. Two-thirds of the families in Putla had members living in another city within the Mexican Republic. Three-quarters of these members now resided in Mexico City; the rest had moved to Oaxaca City, Puebla, Acapulco, Monterrey, Villahermosa, Cuernavaca, Veracruz, Guadalajara, and Ciudad Juárez to work primarily in industries and in jobs spurred by tourism.

Although many left hoping to continue their education and work at the same time, most had to abandon going to school due to lack of money and time. More than half of the Putlecans had family or friends or both to help them get started in their new setting, although many ended up working in the informal market. "I came to Mexico [City] after my husband died. My sister and two of my brothers had moved here before. I needed help to support my kids so my sister offered to let us live with her. It's been difficult. I wanted to learn stenography and typing but there was never enough time. I earn what I can selling *taquitos* [little tacos] outside the house" (Putlecan woman in Mexico City, fifty years old).

For those who remain in Putla, more are employed by commerce and service jobs than work in the primary sector. With the opening of the Escuela Normal in 1979, for the first time people in the district had a chance to study a profession in the residents' hometowns. Ten percent of the working population who live in Putla are teachers. Some teach in the town of Putla, whereas others commute daily or weekly to teach in preschools and in elementary schools throughout the district and in neighboring districts.

The tradition of commerce in the town has assumed even greater importance over the past decade and a half. Putlecans observe the families that owned commercial enterprises and conclude that they are carrying on "business as usual"—spurring the idea that the impact of the crisis was not as severe for them as it was for most of the population (even though the merchants disagree with this belief). Several families that were once poor now own large stores full of merchandise. Rumors that maybe drug money or "pacts with the devil" were involved have waned as people have come to believe that commerce is the only way to get ahead financially.[4]

The major obstacle to opening a business is raising the necessary capital. With the national crisis, townspeople believe that finding a good job with a decent salary in Mexico is now practically impossible. Siblings and cousins living in Mexico City complain about the lack of jobs, or decent-paying ones, and how expensive the city is. "It's passed now the time when you could get a job in Mexico [City]. My cousins work like dogs there and what do they have? The same as when they left here. No, there's too many people there now and you need more papers to work so that the politicians can make more money and build their fancy homes. They do nothing to help us, they only take" (Putlecan man, early fifties). People have lost what little faith they had in the government and in its ability to resolve the crisis. They look to the north, to the United States, and question Mexico's situation. Numerous Putlecans told me repeatedly, "el peso ya no vale" (the peso is worthless now). "We have everything here—lots of land, water, oil, and all other resources. We work hard yet earn nothing. The peso is worthless. Only dollars have value" (Putlecan man, mid-forties).

Across the U.S. Border

The people of Putla have a long history of migration to the United States, beginning some fifty years ago when U.S. agents of the Bracero Program contracted Putlecan men to work in U.S. agricultural fields. Circular migration to and from the United States became a way of life for many men and their sons who followed in their footsteps. Once in the United States, some Putlecans made contacts with other employers and moved east to live permanently, working in factories and in service jobs in Chicago and New York.

Although Putla has had a relatively high out-migration rate since the 1960s,[5] quantitative and qualitative change has marked migration patterns following the 1982 crisis: the number of people migrating from Putla has more than doubled; many wives and daughters have joined their husbands, fathers, and brothers in their journeys to the United States; young people, both male and female, have begun migrating to the United States on their own, often against the wishes of their parents; and two-thirds of migrants after crossing the border in Tijuana fly directly to the East Coast. Almost 80 percent of the families in Putla have at least one member living temporarily or permanently in the United States. As one young Putlecan man remarked, "In the mid-1980s, the town seemed empty. All my friends from school left for el norte [the United States] convinced that they were going to become rich. They tried to get me to go, but my sister and brother have left here and I couldn't leave my parents alone. Still I wonder what it would be like, you know, to go and live in Atlanti [Atlantic City]. They say it's very nice."

In the past, the bulk of Mexican migrants to the United States worked as agricultural laborers in rural areas.[6] During the last two decades, a shift in destination areas has resulted in more than 80 percent of migrants going to metropolitan areas (Portes and Rumbaut 1990:41). Once established in a U.S. city, Mexican enclaves, like other ethnic communities, serve as magnets for new arrivals from their hometown.

On the East Coast, Putlecan men and women are concentrated in the New York City area, Atlantic City, and other beach towns along the New Jersey coastline.[7] Many Putlecans leave Putla in April or May, work the summer season in the United States, and return in October or November as U.S. beach businesses close for the winter. The summer season corresponds with the rainy season in Putla—a time when there is less work in general in Putla and when people call the town "sad," referring to the lack of social activities and interaction.

Atlantic City has become one of the principal receiving areas in the United States, with thousands of Putlecans now residing there permanently and many more migrating seasonally. When public officials in

New Jersey began a revitalization project in Atlantic City, recruiters in the New York City area encouraged Latin and Asian migrants to move to Atlantic City with promises of better-paying jobs.[8] Several Putlecan families moved early on. After having lived in Atlantic City for more than ten years and having obtained legal residency, they have now opened their own small businesses (several restaurants and a grocery store) in the six-block area known as "Little Putla." The restaurants serve Oaxacan-style food and Mexican sodas. In one restaurant, they bake pan de yema. The grocery store sells a variety of basic foods and goods, including tortillas, *chiles secos* (dried peppers), *crema mexicana* (Mexican heavy cream), *queso cotija* (similar to string cheese), chiles la Morena y San Marcos (Mexican brand of various types of canned peppers), *cobertores* San Marcos (Mexican-made blankets), and other Mexican and Oaxacan products. The owners of the store also act as travel agents, selling national and international airplane tickets. The businesses are doing quite well because there is little competition. Moreover, as Alvarez notes in his research on chile commerce, "The increasing demand for ethnic produce in the urban markets of the United States, as exemplified by the City of Los Angeles, stems from the continued multiplication of immigrant communities settling in urban centers" (R. Alvarez 1994:256). The demand not just for produce but also for other Mexican foods and products has made Putlecan businesses in Atlantic City successful.

Upon arrival in the United States, many Putlecans find work in factories sewing, assembling toys, pressing suits, and so forth, but the work is *pesado* (hard, tedious) and pays little. They try to find other work as quickly as possible. Industrial jobs, including construction, currently employ about a tenth of Putlecans in the United States. Most migrants prefer work in service jobs. More than half are employed as busboys, cooks, dishwashers, and waitresses in restaurants, pizza shops, and bakeries; as maids, gardeners, and janitors in hotels, private homes, and public facilities; and as casino workers. "It's easy to find factory jobs, especially in clothing. I sewed buttons on coats, and they liked my work because I did it fast. But they were very strict, even deducting time when you went to the bathroom. I left after a couple of months. I found a job cleaning houses with a Dominican woman. I made about the same but I was done by the time Patricia [her daughter] got out of school" (Putlecan woman, mid-thirties).

Of the migrants who stay on the West Coast, the majority work in agriculture (in a variety of agricultural jobs in California and in apple and cherry orchards in Oregon and Washington) and the rest in service jobs in and around the Los Angeles area. Most Putlecans have family or friends in the United States who help them get established. Social networks are instrumental in finding work and obtaining work visas. The networks provide general survival information in the new setting and "are at the core of the microstructures that sustain migration over time," integrating people across spaces (Portes and Rumbaut 1990:231). But they can also cause conflict when expectations and social obligations are not met.[9]

Putlecan migrants reported that crossing the U.S.–Mexico border is the most dangerous part of their journeys. Few recounted stories of being in adverse or injurious situations once they arrived at their destinations in the United States. Most migrants who have lived in the United States eagerly expressed how much they enjoyed living there, yet at the same time they did miss Putla. "It's sad to be so far away. I think about what's happening there, all the fiestas. I call my family and they always ask, when am I coming home?" (Putlecan man, late twenties).

Wanting to see their family, friends, and *novios y novias* (boy- and girlfriends) is the most common reason given for the migrants' not staying in the United States permanently. Many dream of transplanting certain aspects of U.S. lifeways to Putla, such as better infrastructure and more jobs, comforts, and material resources. They migrate circularly to realize a part of their dream, such as a home with indoor plumbing.

Although many Putlecans cross the border undocumented, most Putlecans who live on the East Coast do not worry about the police and the U.S. Border Patrol once in the United States. To the contrary, they praise the police for keeping order, helping people, and being honest. "The police work for the people, not against them like in Mexico. If I have a problem I know that I can call them and they will help me" (Putlecan man, mid-twenties). Their perceptions are strikingly different from Putlecan migrants who go to the West Coast. They fear the police and worry about the INS deporting them, because it costs them a couple of days of work and extra money to reenter the United States and to travel back up the West Coast. Their comments are sim-

ilar to those made by Mexican migrants living in California as reported by Rouse (1992).[10]

Many migrants report that Social Security cards and work visas are
relatively easy to obtain, especially for casino employees in Atlantic
City. Recreational activities, such as going to the movies, parties, clubs,
restaurants, the beach, and parks, are limited more by financial constraints rather than by a concern for *la migra* (the INS). The Mexican-
American Unity Council has expanded beyond New York City to form a
southern New Jersey branch. The council organizes sports programs
and social events for Mexicans living in the United States. Participation
in sports programs is high and helps unify Putlecans and other
Mexicans in a foreign country.[11]

Remittances

While working in the United States, two-thirds of migrants send remittances to their parents or spouses in Putla, although the frequency
and amount vary substantially.[12] The majority of remittances are used
for food and family maintenance (clothing, health supplies, kids'
school supplies, party supplies, and so on), house construction, and
consumer goods. The largest local furniture and appliance store
owner in the town of Putla told me that when he first opened in the
mid-1980s, he sold beds and more beds. Today, beds and wardrobes are
still his top-selling items, followed by kitchen appliances: blenders,
stoves, and refrigerators. His sales correspond with remittance expenditures reported to me in the survey of the community. People first
buy bedroom furniture, followed by kitchen appliances, and lastly, sofa
sets for the living room. Few people still sleep on petates, but ham-
mocks continue to be the most popular living room seat.

Many migrants have saved to open a *tienda de abarrotes* (little grocery store). Some have used their money to purchase livestock or land.
Several Putlecans who worked as cooks in restaurants in the United
States have used their new skills to open restaurants with a "gringo"
flavor, offering Sunday "all-you-can-eat" buffets or adding pizzas and
other atypical foods to their menu. Several provide catering services.

"I first went to D.F. [the Federal District] with my brother and worked
in an elegant restaurant in Polanco.[13] But there was a problem and I
left. Then I got the chance to go to New York, and I worked in several
restaurants for over eight years until I saved enough to open this one.

I learned a lot there, and I've got lots of ideas for making my restaurant very special, like this buffet" (Putlecan man, mid-thirties).

Before the 1990s, a few tiendas de abarrotes dotted the streets. The town now has hundreds of them (most sponsored by migrant capital) in which one can buy canned goods, snacks, sodas, beer, liquors, dairy products, cigarettes, household goods (light bulbs, candles, soaps, detergents, lotions, and so forth) and other national-brand products. The stores are run primarily by women who can tend the store and do household duties at the same time because the stores are located in the homes. In the smaller shops, customers tend to be neighbors, friends, and relatives who yell for the owner as they enter the stores. In other larger stores, immediate and extended family members take turns attending the clients; a few hire nonfamily salespersons.

Profits are minimal for most store owners. After the initial investment, migrants' remittances are often needed to restock the shelves. The smaller stores are more a form of savings than profit generating because families invest remittances in products that they use, such as household goods and snacks. They save money by not purchasing these items at another store for a higher cost and by converting their money into consumer goods, protecting themselves against inflation or monetary devaluations. Women can support their families during their husband's absences or between remittances by consuming store items and by using the few pesos earned through sales to buy other essentials.[14] The larger stores, on the other hand, generate a greater income, depend less on remittances, and provide the "model" for many smaller store owners, whose goal is to increase the amount and variety of goods sold so that their commercial enterprises can support their families and end their need for migration.

It is these goals that conflict with the message of the local ecology group. Although people agree that trash is a major community problem, they consider the solution proposed by the ecology group, to stop buying packaged goods, an attack on merchants' and shopkeepers' livelihoods. When the priest tells the people to stop sucking their *mamila* (referring to the drinking of sodas in plastic bags with straws), store owners see pesos flying out the door. The growth in the number of tiendas de abarrotes due to migrant remittances has made competition fierce. Store owners fear that if they stop selling sodas in a bag, customers will go to another store to get them. Sodas and snacks constitute an important part of daily sales in many stores.

Some families that own pasturelands invest remittances in livestock. Livestock products yield a greater profit than crops. For hundreds of years the region has supported the production of both crops and livestock, but in the past two decades there has been greater pressure to convert farming lands into pasturelands—a practice observed in other rural Mexican communities (Reichert 1981; Mines and Massey 1985; Dinerman 1982). In the late 1970s, only four or five stalls in the market in Putla were *carniceros* (butchers); by 1994 butchers occupied forty-five stalls. The growth in vendors is due not only to market incentives and the infusion of U.S. dollars into the local economy but also to the belief that meat and other livestock products are more healthful than vegetables and fish. Mothers worry about having enough milk for their children to drink daily. Beef, the most expensive meat per kilogram, is also a status symbol. Wealthier Putlecans comment on the fact that they eat beef every day and would never have a fiesta without serving it as the main dish.

Besides sending remittances, migrants return from the United States with a variety of consumer goods, especially electronic equipment. Most Putlecans return from their first stay in the United States with at least a new television or new clothes, and from subsequent trips VCRs, boom boxes, stereos, video cameras, and other consumer items. Even migrants from the poorest families have brought back televisions. While conducting my interviews, rarely a week passed that I was not asked to translate manuals for electronic equipment or other consumer goods; my greatest challenge was directing the assembly of a Nautilus weight-lifting machine. Most migrants desire to buy a car or a truck, although only a few save enough to purchase a vehicle and to pay the taxes for Mexican license plates upon their return. More often, migrants who work seasonally in the United States circumvent buying Mexican plates by reregistering their vehicles every six months at the U.S.–Mexico border. The increase of modern consumer goods coupled with the influx of U.S. dollars in Putla has resulted in many changes in the community, not only material changes but also in the beliefs of the Putlecans.

"The More, the Better"

In the late 1980s and early 1990s, *coyotes* (smugglers) in Tijuana charged approximately 3,000 new pesos (U.S.$1000) to smuggle a person across the border and fly him or her to New York from San Diego, although some Putlecans have paid as much as 5,000 new pesos when more stringent border control operations were in effect. Fees charged to cross the border only ranged from U.S.$200 to $700.

Research shows that more than half of the undocumented Mexican migrants to the United States are not impoverished peasants but rather urban dwellers who are literate, many having at least some secondary schooling (Portes and Rumbaut 1990:11). The backgrounds of U.S.–destined Putlecans coincide with the national figures. Most have completed junior high school. Few migrants are from the poorest segment of the Putlecan population because members of that group are unable to raise the necessary resources to make a journey. Class plays an important role not only in differentiating who will come to the United States, but also in influencing their choice of destination area. For the most part, migrants from families with greater resources fly to the East Coast, whereas those with less remain on the West Coast. Primarily working in agriculture, migrants on the West Coast earn less than those working in service jobs on the East Coast but their initial investment is less also. However, in terms of the amount invested compared to family resources available, both groups partake in investment and risk, especially first-time migrants, who most likely have borrowed the money for their journey from relatives or friends.

It is not absolute deprivation but rather relative deprivation that drives migration (Cornelius 1977; Portes and Rumbaut 1990). As the world becomes "smaller" via advances in technology, people living in "third" world countries have become increasingly aware of living standards in industrialized countries and of the economic opportunities absent in their own.

For skilled workers and small farmers, migration is the means to stabilize family livelihoods and meet long-desired aspirations—a car, a TV set, domestic appliances of all sorts, additional land and implements. For urban professionals, it provides a means of reaching life standards commensurate with their past achievements and to progress in their careers. Seen from this perspective, contemporary immigration is a direct consequence of the dominant influence attained by the culture of the advanced West in every corner of the globe. The bewildering number and variety of today's immigrants reflect this worldwide reach and the vision of modern life and individual fulfillment that goes with it.

(Portes and Rumbaut 1990:13)

Many teachers in Putla have requested a year of leave to see what opportunities they can find in the United States.[15] Many who have done well financially in the United States have abandoned teaching as a career, replacing it with circular migration as the means of earning a living. "Our salaries are miserable; you can't afford to buy your children the little things that they ask for and then you feel bad," explained one teacher. Many of these teachers have saved their income earned in the United States and have started their own commercial businesses or have joined with family members in their Putlecan enterprises. Others have returned to teaching after their journeys to the United States. As another teacher noted, "Yes, I made more money in el norte, but I missed my family too much. Children need their father or else they will start getting into trouble." Often a family's emotional needs take precedence over economic concerns, although almost everyone is constantly seeking new ways to increase income. Families in which both the wife and the husband teach, thus achieving a higher level of income and security through their combined positions, rarely migrate.

Putlecan women and men living in the United States witness and experience new ways of living. For many, it is the first time they live in a home equipped with indoor plumbing and numerous modern appliances—refrigerator, stove, microwave, dishwasher, washing machine, and so on. Putlecan women comment on how much easier life is for women in the United States, "who have machines to do all their work." Earning dollars, migrants have more buying power. They judge how successful their journey has been by listing all the consumer goods they have purchased. As a Putlecan in Atlantic City stated, "My nephew works as a waiter and now owns a new car and lots of expensive clothes. We're very proud of him."

Several women remarked on how cheaply one can buy "nice" things shopping at yard sales in the United States. The abundance of consumer goods coupled with relatively inexpensive prices turn most migrants into eager shoppers—not all, however, because personal habits affect one's money management. Migrants who "drink all their money" or who "don't know how to save" are a source of family disgrace. These migrants express remorse for not helping the family. The social pressure to send remittances is so strong that some Putlecans in Atlantic City state that they cannot return to Putla, not even for a visit, because they have not sent their families any money or goods. For some Putlecan men, these feelings have kept them in the United States for more than ten years. They have yet to save any money. As one man admitted to me, "Yes, I do drink a lot. And I can't return to my family poorer than when I left. I would rather die here alone than hurt my family's honor."

Migration uproots people from their families and their communities and from their conventional ways of understanding the world. They enter a new terrain filled with new people, new images, new lifeways, and new experiences. They return from urban centers in the Mexican Republic or from the United States and act as agents of change. Arriving with different ideas and material goods, they stimulate the desire for the consumption of "modern" goods, that is, national and international consumer goods. The urban-Western way of life is reconstructed as superior to the "backward" ways of life in the rural Mexican provinces. Part of this inference of superiority is connected to beliefs that equate "modernity" and "progress" with increased consumption of material goods. Migrants reinforce these constructions with their stories about the United States and its vast array of material goods and resources.

Information and Expansion of Technologies

To portray migrants as the sole cause of increasing consumption in Putla would be too simplistic. Although I do argue that they are responsible for stimulating much of the desire for increasing consumption, they are one of several sources of the transmission of new ideas and of the yearning for new material resources and consumer goods. Public education, the mass media, and other new technologies are also sources that have actively promoted and supported changes in Putlecan attitudes and consumption activities.

Public Education

From the Mexican Revolution to the mid twentieth century, the government promoted national unity, particularly in its education policies. Officially, the role of education was to "form a nationalist spirit" and to be "devoid of all foreign influence" (Lacy 1994:234). However, after World War II, the official stance began to change and policy followed the pronouncements of international agencies, particularly the United Nations Education, Scientific and Cultural Organization (UNESCO) (Lacy 1994:235). Education became tied to the government's goals of economic and social development. Literacy campaigns were accompanied by community improvement activities, such as agricultural and livestock programs, health care, road building, and construction of homes and community centers. In the 1950s, the government began building thousands of new schools and training thousands of new teachers, giving priority to technical and vocational education allied with national development plans (Lacy 1994:236). Modernization theories have accompanied nationalistic ideologies in educational policies for some forty years.

In the list of educational objectives published by the Secretary of Public Education (SEP) in 1993, the goal "to teach national values and love of country" remains, but rather than scorning "foreign influences" the government promotes the "understanding of diverse national and international processes" that have made Mexico the country that it is today (SEP 1993:14). The general guidelines for education and the guidelines for teaching stated in school textbooks emphasize the need to develop strong "individuals" who will help the country "develop" into a more Westernlike nation. "Resolver esos problemas (la pobreza, el deterioro de la ecología, democracia, economía) es tarea de los mexicanos de hoy. . . . Es la historia que te toca vivir y hacer, cambiar y mejorar. Es tu lugar en la historia de México" (SEP 1992:79).[16]

The fostering of individualism (as opposed to communalism) has played a pivotal role in changing students' attitudes and practices. In Putla, parents complain of their children's lack of respect for elders and their declaration of "rights" that they learn in school—their right to playtime or their right to toys and snacks. A Putlecan mother compares childhoods of different generations: "Children today don't have to help out the family like we did as kids. We had to get up before sunrise and do many chores. We never questioned our parents. We did what we were told to do. Kids today, they have it easy, too easy, if you ask me. Not only do they not listen, sometimes they even tell me what to do!"

The spread of the federal rural school system magnified educational differences across generations because it brought about participation of children from all classes in formal education and increased the number of years of schooling.[17] The changes in the structure and content of formal schooling have helped shape differences in attitudes and practices of the younger generation by providing knowledge of an alternative way of life: the urban-Western way of life. As discussed in chapter 3, a contradiction persists between official national educational policies, which on paper endorse the multicultural Mexico and which in practice try to streamline students into "one" Mexico—a modern, more Westernlike nation.

As Gramsci (1971) pointed out, it is in the arena of civil society that consent to certain forms of domination is produced, and public education in Mexico has played a pivotal role in shaping everyday reasoning. This is not to say that all students are programmed to be "ideal" citizens but that they have internalized certain ideas about "modernity" and "progress." Some students in the higher levels of education, such as the COBAO and the Escuela Normal in Putla, learn to critique their government's actions as failing to adhere to the ideals of participatory democracy. They call for the end of corrupt, paternalistic practices. But few students I interviewed rebuked Mexico's overall development plan and economic goals.[18] Most students told me that they wish that Mexico "were more like the United States" and that someday they would like to own a "big" house with modern appliances, a "new car," and "lots of clothes."

Public education provides much of the schooling for Putlecans but children and adults today learn as much, if not more, outside the walls of the classroom. The steady deluge of information, images, ideas, and attitudes from modern media places "education" within the expanding systems of global communication. Multiple mass media sources—

news coverage, magazines, comic books, advertising, popular music, television, film—supply information that directly influences people's everyday thoughts and actions.

Mass Media

With the rapid global expansion of technology and communication systems, the mass media has begun to penetrate people's lives as never before. In Putla, watching television has become the most popular leisure activity, replacing visitation of friends and relatives, the most common activity some twenty years ago. New technologies, such as VCRs, satellite dishes, and computers, have brought national and transnational imagery to homes in what were once relatively isolated areas. With marketing and propaganda strategies, new messages are quickly and easily dispersed to the general public.

Mass media first appeared in Putla in the form of film during the 1930s. The cinema was so popular that the family who owned and ran the theater opened a second theater, Cine Mundo, by 1965. During this time—the "golden age" of Mexican cinema—actors and actresses, such as Jorge Negrete, Dolores del Río, Pedro Armendáriz, María Félix, Mario Moreno Cantinflas, and Pedro Infante, captured the hearts and minds of Putlecans, the same effect they had on most Mexicans. People followed the cinema closely and shared the frustrations and desires of their idols.

More than simple entertainment, the cinema offered "itself as a unifying space where the deep convictions of the audience coexist[ed] with the beliefs imposed by modernity" (Monsiváis 1985:239). It became another source of national unity, incorporating the illiterate masses into the nation-state in a way that education alone could never do. "The cinema is a crucial element in the process of national integration. Its importance increases because of its status as intermediary between a victorious State and the masses who, lacking any democratic tradition, find in their sentimental education their most visible source of unity" (239).

The foundation of Mexican cinema re-created the idea of the nation as an extension of the family (Monsiváis 1985:239). The nationalist focus helped to reinforce nationalistic themes in education, in political campaigns, in economic policies (such as import substitution), and so forth during this time. But soon the cinema and its nationalist sentiments would compete with another form of mass entertainment: the television.

During the 1970s in Putla, the popularity of the cinema was slowly replaced by the introduction of television and later by VCRs.[19] Television program content in Mexico has been commercial in nature. Mexico has only one public station (out of twenty-four), and access to that station is limited to urban areas. The town of Putla receives one station, Televisa.[20] The programs and practices of Televisa are heavily influenced by U.S. broadcasting corporations (ABC, NBC)—as are most Latin American television companies—because these U.S. corporations own major interests in Latin American companies. The companies imitate U.S. programming styles, purchase U.S. programs, and copy U.S. advertising practices. Their main emphasis is "the sale of modern sector goods" (Wells 1994:208). "Program content, the linkages with advertising and U.S. consumer manufacturers and the strong commercial nature of the operations in general, are each contributing factors which fashion the medium into a powerful conduit for widespread consumerism" (203).[21]

Ninety-three percent of Putlecans own a television and typically spend three to six hours daily watching it.[22] Due to the limited channel reception, satellite dishes are becoming popular in the town, with a total of ninety-four dishes atop of people's homes in 1994. Television is a key site of information, images, and debates from which people make sense of the world. Television programming does not simply reflect lifeways; it delivers "careful, deliberate constructions" (Douglas 1994:16). The messages and images produced are often contradictory, dramatizing or magnifying certain features of life while ignoring or collapsing others.[23] The television programmers' goal is to reach as many people as possible, and they often offer homogenized, romanticized images that can be inconsistent with what is happening in the daily lives of people.

Half of the women in Putla who told me that they follow the night *telenovelas* (soap operas) believe that life in Putla is like life in those novelas. While watching a soap, a Putlecan woman commented, "Maybe Putla doesn't have all those fancy homes and cars and we aren't rich like they [the characters] are, but we face the same problems. You know, husbands fooling around, even wives too, like María in the market who. . ." She, like many others, identifies with the characters' lives, disregarding their differences and envisioning problems as being the same for everyone. Not all soap opera watchers share this view, however. About a third of Putlecan women, both young and old, who watch soap operas believe that the shows are pure fiction. They watch them because they appear on the only channel available.

Putlecans, except for satellite dish owners, receive almost all current news from television, and their main news source is *24 Horas* (24 Hours) on Televisa. Although privately owned, the news program is pro PRI government and one-sided in its reporting.[24] Alternative interpretations of current events can be found in some newspapers. Only a few of the Putlecans I interviewed reported reading a newspaper, however. Of those who did, about half read *Excelsior* from Mexico City (also pro-PRI) and the rest read the Oaxacan paper, *El Imparcial,* for more regional news coverage.

The programs and commercials on television reinforce and elaborate the ideas of consumer capitalism. Images and symbols of luxury and abundance and of privilege and franchise are reproduced on the screen. These images seduce people into believing that by purchasing a particular hair product or detergent or brand of clothes they can join the ranks of the elite. Most of the media stars are light skinned, as are the advertising models, suggesting that one can "whiten" one's skin by using "modern" consumer goods. Children in Putla are especially influenced by cartoons and by toy ads. They tell their parents they "need" Ninja Turtles or Barbies or mega plastic trucks and that they cannot live without a certain brand of *papitas* (potato chips) or candies.

The newest addition to mass media sources in Putla is the town's radio station, Radio 890 A.M. XEPOR, founded in 1991. Almost every Putlecan family owns a radio, and most people listen to it regularly. The station is commercial, selling advertising time to local merchants and national companies, and is staffed primarily with Putlecans from wealthier families who have received degrees in journalism, communications, or marketing from universities in Mexico City. The program content also includes news and modern music. The owner of the station brings in popular groups from Acapulco and Mexico City for an annual money-making concert. Held outside on the large coffee-drying patio, the event is a time for wealthier Putlecans (especially those who work at the station) to display the latest fashions. Women dress in

elegant evening gowns, spiked heels, and gold jewelry they have purchased outside of Putla; the men dress more casually. Poorer
Putlecans stand outside the chain-link fence watching the display,
many wishing they were inside. But as one woman asked, "Even if we
could afford to buy tickets, what would I wear? I'd be embarrassed to
wear my best dress. Next to them [the other women], it would look like
a rag."

More than 2,500 people attended the concert in November 1993, but
the owner complained of low attendance and blamed the townspeople for being ignorant about "good" music rather than recognizing
how cost prohibitive it was for most of them. Although community
members listen to contemporary Mexican and U.S. pop music all the
time, blaring it out of their homes or cars for all to hear, the most popular concert-festivals are those in which La Furia Oaxaqueña play.
"When we have dances to make money for the school, we always try
to get La Furia because everyone will come" (Putlecan woman, early
forties). A Putlecan-based band, La Furia plays regional music, highlighted by *chilenas,* a regional-style music and dance known for its
zapateo (rapid feet-stomping). Putlecans love to *zapatear.* [25]

Magazines are another mass media source growing in popularity.
The main newsstand owner told me that sales have been rising slowly
but steadily in the last ten years. A little more than half the people in
my survey reported buying magazines regularly. The most popular
magazines, such as *Eres, Estrellas, TVnovelas, Somos, Televista, Mujer,
TV-Guía, Furia,* and *Chico,* are about television, movie, or musical
stars. Home, cooking and dieting, and women's magazines, such as
Cosmopolitan, Vanidades, Activa, Oye, 15 a 20, Hogares, Ideas, Kena,
and *Dietas,* are read earnestly by Putlecan women ranging from
teenagers to women in their mid-thirties and by some men.
Magazines dealing with history, politics, or current affairs and professional journals are read primarily by teachers and other professionals
and by some people with education beyond the elementary level.
Some Putlecans subscribe to *Selecciones* (*Reader's Digest* in Spanish),
and a small minority receive Catholic magazines.

The images and advertisements in magazines (except the religious
ones) are similar to those in television. They appeal to people by
showing what is "modern" and "progressive." Several readers told me

that magazines teach them what is *a la moda* (in style). Many times I watched young women sit and discuss new fashions or hairdos page by page. The ads for national-brand, and more recently U.S.–brand, products try to convince readers how much better their lives would be if they bought brand X or ate processed cheese. No "modern" woman is "complete" without Tupperware: "quieres saber como mejorará tu vida con Tupperware, llámanos hoy mismo" (to find out how to make your life better with Tupperware, call us today). Glass, plastic, and metal containers are depicted as "superior" and more sanitary than locally produced pottery. "Vitro Envases Norteamérica: Por ser el material más higiénico por excelencia, el vidrio mantiene intactas las propiedades de los productos. . . . Además el vidrio se recicla. Compare y luego consuma. Verá que el vidrio es la mejor opción" (Advertisement in *TVnovelas* 15[23]:37).[26] Advertisers throw in English words to show their "first"-worldliness: "Dico Muebles con aplicación safety shield" (Dico furniture with an upholstery protective spray) or "Con Modern Schools adquiera una formación en la comodidad de su hogar" (with Modern Schools acquire an education in the comfort of your home).

As new products arrive in Putla, women have begun to experiment with different vegetables and fruits such as broccoli and apples. Recipes for "modern" cuisine call for a wider range of foods, especially processed foods, and for new kitchen appliances. For example, blenders have become a "basic" necessity for cooking. When I told some women that I prefer to use a *molcajete* (stone bowl with grinding stone), rather than a blender, to make salsa, they thought I was crazy.

Other New Technology

Computer classes are now offered in the town, taught privately by a Putlecan who studied computer science in Mexico City. With about a dozen computers, his classes stay full. Teachers encourage students to obtain computer skills, and most young people in the COBAO and Escuela Normal consider computer training necessary for "getting ahead." Several professional people own personal computers. Younger professional people were very interested in my laptop, and I was frequently asked for my opinion on various models and software programs.

The telephone has become a vital link between family members in Putla and those who have migrated. Two hundred and fifteen families have private lines; many more have placed orders and are waiting to be connected. Several families with tiendas de abarrotes offer phone service to clients for a fee, and there is one public phone service in the center of town. Families without phones arrange specific times for their kin outside of Putla to call them at one of these stores. The local radio station is also used as a medium to connect relatives. The person outside Putla will call the radio station and tell the deejay what time and where he or she will call a particular family member; the deejay announces the message on air. FAX machines also link a few Putlecan businesspeople, government officials, and branches of national banks with the outside world.

Consumption

The fostering of the consumption of urban-Western goods in the region of Putla has been supported by the "modernizing" attitude spread by migrants, public education, the mass media, and other new technologies. Although a gap exists between the economic reality of most families and their ability to buy, their list of desired goods continues to grow. Market integration has generated a vast spectrum of change in people's daily lives. As Arizpe (1981:633) observes, market integration has resulted in a "total reordering of economic and social relations" throughout Mexico.

Declining production, the diminished use of goods produced locally or regionally, the rise of cash needs for new services and goods, the increasing mobility of family members, and the growth of individualism have led to greater social and economic inequalities within families and within the community. Some community members are disenfranchised from the consumer culture with little hope of ever buying more than the basic necessities for survival. Others, no longer satisfied with their social position, devise various strategies to earn more money and more prestige through consumptive display. Migration is one such strategy and used by numerous people to attain their goals. Wealthier Putlecans use their social and economic capital to amass more goods for conspicuous consumption. As Tomlinson (1990:9) points out, "The commodity has acquired, in late consumer capitalism, an aura beyond just its function. The commodity now acts on the consumer, endows him/her with perceived qualities which can be displayed in widening public contexts. . . . It is the difference between buying an object mainly for its function, and acquiring an item for its style. Motor cars or jeans, for instance, are produced and consumed as more than functional means of mobility or clothing."

Although it may seem that the urban-Western lifestyle rules in the hearts and minds of the people, it is certainly not exempted from criticism. People who brag about the things they have, those who refuse to help in community fiestas, or those who return with a handful of cash ready to party and race around in their New Jersey–tagged cars are subjected to gossip and slander by community members. Putlecans who remain in the town scorn those who return with stories of how they "live like kings" in the United States. A young man stopped me on the street one day to "help me with my research" and gave me a five-minute speech on how "most" U.S.–destined Putlecans end up with nothing and how the town would be better off if people stayed and "developed what we have here."[27] Furthermore, when I asked people what they would do if they received an abundance of money, half said they would spend it on someone other than themselves, either to help *los pobres* (the poor) and *los huérfanos* (orphans) or to "improve the community" by providing better public services and infrastructure, more recreational activities, and bigger community festivals.

As consumerism expands, people invest more in the private sphere. The importance of the local community does not, however, automatically disintegrate simply because one invests more in material goods or because one no longer lives in the community. Migrants who have lived in New Jersey for many years still call Putla "home." Between 1990 and 1993, twenty couples who currently live in California and New Jersey returned to Putla to have their babies baptized; this practice is even more common for Putlecans who live in the Mexican Federal District. Outside Putla, migrants still serve as mayordomos by mailing their share of the expenses. El Carnaval, the largest town festival, has been growing in size and in content over the past two decades. When several disgruntled Putlecans in 1994 complained of the growing appearance of factory-made costumes and foreign themes,[28] mayordomos pushed for the return to traditional straw and clay masks and costumes. Many responded. Putlecans living in the United States have also sent money for the church restoration project. From 1990 to 1993, the restoration committee raised over U.S.$80,000 to renovate the church and office buildings. The priest had no exact figures on how much money Putlecan migrants have sent, but he said they have contributed a notable amount. The priest announces the names of people who have given money each week in the Sunday Mass. Migrants renew their social ties to the community through such practices.

Some Putlecans resist what they perceive as the rigid control of their time while they are in the United States. "You earn better, but you never stop working" and "all you do is work" were frequent comments about the working conditions in the United States. For them, the pace of life is slower and more appealing in Putla. Although people recognize that one must earn a living, the need for money does not solely drive their decisions about migration.

Putla is a commercial town and has been an important marketplace in western Oaxaca since pre-Hispanic times. Consumption of goods beyond basic necessities is not necessarily evil; nor are people passive pawns of advertisers' wiles. Many goods have made life a little easier for people, such as blenders and tortilla-making machines, which have reduced some labor time for women. After my first time scrubbing my own clothes on a stone washboard, I wished that I could give every wife a washing machine. Telephones have allowed family members to stay in touch in a way the Mexican postal system never could. Several professional people commented that without cars, satellite dishes, and computers they probably would not have returned to Putla after studying in Mexico City, because they would have felt too isolated, too out of touch with the rest of the world. If they had not returned, the community would have lost much-needed medical knowledge and other skills. Increasing consumption can have both negative and positive effects. Douglas and Isherwood (1979:12) sum it up: "Goods are neutral, their uses are social; they can be used as bridges or fences."

The lack of investment of migrant remittances in productive activities that could lead to greater local development versus the spending of money on consumption has been a focus of scholarly debate. The economies of many communities throughout Mexico have become dependent on migrant remittances (Grindle 1988). This dependence process has been described as *nortenización* (R. Alarcón 1988), "migration syndrome" (Reichert 1981), "relay migration" (Arizpe 1982), and "crisis-induced, income-maintenance migration" (Cornelius 1978:29). Migrants have been called "economic refugees" (Stuart and Kearney 1981:7). Lack of employment, economic development, and a productive base place Putla among towns dependent on migration.

Most small commercial businesses (mainly tiendas de abarrotes) in which a majority of remittances are invested still require remittance infusions after their initial establishment. Store owners are fully aware that their businesses depend on *migradólares* (migration dollars). Restaurant and bar owners earn almost all of their annual income in the three winter months when many migrants return or when they normally send greater numbers of remittances.[29] The infusion of U.S. dollars into the local economy has resulted in local prices' rising faster than the national average. Land prices and rents have skyrocketed. Lots sell for more in Putla than in middle-class neighborhoods in Oaxaca City.[30] The planting of traditional crops continues to decline as more land is used for livestock. As Mines and Massey (1985:116–117) note, many migrants are absentee landlords who consider any income earned in their home community as supplemental to their migration earnings. The same sense of home production as subordinate to migration earnings is true in Putla for some migrants who invest in livestock, purchasing animals one by one and underusing lands until they can afford more livestock. In order to buy more animals, they continue to migrate. The construction industry, which employs numerous in-migrants and is the only booming industry in Putla, is supported primarily by remittances.

Remittances heighten dependence on migration because most are used for food, housing, and consumer goods. Researchers have tended to emphasize the negative effects of this process—the dependency and lack of development fostered by out-migration. But this emphasis on the structural results overlooks individual actions and the reasons for social-spending patterns. Obviously, food is necessary to survival, but what about other expenditures in housing or consumer goods?

As land and rent prices rise, agricultural production declines, and people seek cash-generating activities, most Putlecans have only their home and lot as spaces in which to invest. Families build two-story homes to rent extra bedrooms to boarders, to set up their tiendas de abarrotes on the first floor, and to accommodate growing extended families because many newlyweds cannot afford to buy, build, or rent their own homes. Housing is an important repository of investment. Furthermore, as Heyman shows, the replacement of locally made construction materials (adobe, cane, and mud roofs) with more expensive, more durable, externally manufactured materials (cement blocks, galvanized sheet metal roofs) saves families time and money in the long run and allows them to take "an active role toward their social standing when in the past the status referents had largely been rigid" (Heyman 1994:134).

Durand and Massey (1992:28) point out that most migration studies that examine expenditures fail to take into account the life-cycle stage of the people involved. The largest group of migrants are younger (between eighteen and forty). Their circular migration corresponds to the time when couples are having their own families. "During this phase of the life cycle, demands for family maintenance, housing and medical care are greatest, and it is not surprising that migrants channel most of their earnings into current consumption" (Durand and Massey 1992:28). Later on in life, as families mature and children become adults, migrants invest more in productive activities than in consumption (28). Both of these tendencies are true for migrants in Putla. Several Putlecans who began migrating as braceros and then continued as undocumented workers after the program ended used remittances for family maintenance for some fifteen to twenty years. Only after most of their children were grown did they begin investing in commercial enterprises, such as butcher shops or cement-pipe manufacturing businesses.

Crossing Borders

Consumption is a social process, one that channels resources and draws lines of social relationships. When migrants send remittances to families back home, they are helping their families materially but they are also maintaining and renewing their social relationships, their connections with their home community. "Material goods are embedded in social relations" (Glick, Schiller, Basch, and Blanc-Szanton 1992:10). They speak to the social success of their kin living in new contexts and link the fabric of daily life across borders.

Migration integrates families across geographic and cultural borders. These connections provide individuals and families access to new forms of information and resources used in everyday decision-making processes. New information, technologies, and resources create new patterns of differentiation on material and social levels. Consumption becomes a critical factor in these patterns and in definitions of the self. It permeates our bodies, the spaces in which we live, our daily activities. Even when people remain rooted in one place, changes in beliefs and actions occur between generations. But as people move between spaces, change comes with increasing speed. New constructions of identity emerge in the migration process, mediated by global political and economic environments.

5

Constructing, Contesting, Defending Identities

What hurts Indians most is that our costumes are considered beautiful, but it's as if the person wearing it didn't exist.

(Rigoberta Menchú 1984:204)

Urban migration is the prime way to "move up" within the rural hometown but simultaneously, within the cities where they go to live, most people from rural peasant backgrounds find themselves back down on the lowest rung of the ladder.

(Turino 1993:28)

*t*he town of Putla is largely inhabited by mestizos and families descended from the hacienda landholding class, both of whom collectively refer to themselves as *gente de razón* (civilized people).[1] The wealthier landholding families have maintained their economic, political, and social power in the town and district, even though some of their lands have been redistributed during this century. Besides owning land, these families have inherited and expanded lucrative commercial enterprises, controlling most of the buying and selling of commodities throughout the region.[2] They dominate political affairs to the point that few other Putlecans of voting age are politically active.[3]

One of the greatest shocks to wealthier Putlecan women and men who migrate within the Mexican Republic is their reception by strangers in the new place. Called *oaxaquitos* (meaning little Indians) by city residents, especially by those from the nation's capital, Putlecans feel the discrimination and racism that they themselves direct toward indigenous people in and around their hometown. Their class and ethnic identities become homogenized as "poor Indian" through the identification of their birthplace, the state of Oaxaca. By changing spaces, they lose what Adams (1975) calls "social power"—their ability "to use the things that they control in order to have their way in spite of the resistance of others" (Turino 1993:25). Their display of urban-Western clothing, homes, and cars to mark their wealth and power in the hometown becomes muted in the city. The practice by many wealthier Putlecans of finding non-Putlecan spouses and boy- or girl-friends to differentiate themselves becomes pointless in a city where almost everyone is from some other place.

Changing spaces and negotiating borders are practices that re-create forms of self-identification as well as the identities of outsiders. Migrants entering a new terrain not only encounter "others" who are strangers but begin to realize that they too are seen as strangers (R. Williams 1958:299–300). New tools of negotiation are required as migrants learn how to represent themselves in the new context with the marketplace of consumer goods as their main guide. The constructions are contested terrain (Glick, Schiller, Basch, and Blanc-Szanton 1992:4–5). Not only the migrants but the leading class forces have a stake in these constructions because capitalist profits from migrant labor depend on the establishment and maintenance of efficient discriminatory ideologies (Meillassoux [1975] 1981).

The migration process is inherently political. In the course of defining and redefining their "selves," migrants compete for economic and symbolic capital,[4] and reproduce themselves as political and social subjects. In this chapter, I examine how Putlecan women and men create, modify, and defend their constructions of identity, and I explore these constructions along several of the major axes of social relations: ethnicity, "race," gender, class, sexuality, and religion. Social relations shape the processes of socioeconomic differentiation, which in turn shape social relations—a feedback process.

Ethnic and Racial Relations

Peoples' sense of self is grounded in space and in time. When migrating to the United States for the first time, Putlecans discover that they are lumped together with other Spanish-speaking people and are referred to as "Hispanics" by the dominant society. Putlecans never use this term to refer to themselves and resist this homogenization.[5] They recognize the differences in nationalities and in historical experiences of those comprising the ethnic category Hispanic. They say with pride that they are *mexicanos/as* (Mexican) or, among Mexicans, that they are *oaxaqueños/as* (Oaxacans). Men play on local soccer teams with other Putlecans and Mexicans against their rivals: *salvadoreños* (Salvadoreans), *colombianos* (Colombians), *peruanos* (Peruvians), and so forth. Putlecan women and men identify other Latin American people with whom they work by their nationality, for example, el Guatemalteco (the Guatemalan). Like other Latin American immigrants, Putlecans recognize their shared linguistic and cultural roots with other Latins, but this recognition seldom serves to create a feeling of Latin American unity or oneness. "National experiences are too divergent and national loyalties too deeply embedded to yield to this supranational logic" (Portes and Rumbaut 1990:137).

Living in working-class neighborhoods in the United States that have higher poverty and crime rates, many Putlecans associate darker skin color with unacceptable behaviors, such as theft, drug and alcohol use, prostitution, and gangs. Their world becomes further turned upside down when they encounter paisanos who do not extend what they have grown up to define as normal customs of hospitality. Acts on the part of others such as pretending not to speak Spanish, failing to loan money, closing the door when one needs a place to stay, and negating other ways of giving a helping hand have caused Putlecans to be wary of their fellow Mexicans and angry at some Putlecans who have now settled in the United States.[6]

> I couldn't believe when they [two Putlecan women] said they didn't have room for me. We were best friends in school and now they acted as if they hardly knew me. Finally they said I could stay for a couple of days while I looked for a place, but the situation was very uncomfortable. A woman at the church helped me [find a place], even though she didn't know me. She even gave me some furniture. You all [white North Americans] are good people.
>
> (Putlecan woman, twenty-six years old)

When I asked how often Chicanos refused to speak Spanish and why, a Putlecan woman answered, "Oh, it's real common for them to pretend that they don't speak Spanish. It makes them feel superior. But even I could tell that their English wasn't like the way you speak. They think they're so cool, but I'd tell them they're stupid, and I leave."

Putlecans who have migrated to the New York City and New Jersey areas told me repeatedly that one cannot trust someone just because he or she speaks the same language, especially Puerto Ricans.

> I was working alone in a pizzeria [in Atlantic City] and as soon as I saw them [group of Puerto Rican youths], I knew there would be trouble so I called the police. Lucky I did because from the moment they entered they started *haciendo desmadre* [causing problems]—turning tables over, cursing, throwing stuff—and

then they began threatening me. Was I happy to see the police arrive. Who knows what they would have done next. You know, I had to call the police three different times because of these kids.

(Putlecan man, fifty-six years old)

Gang violence and drug use frighten many Putlecan mothers when their sons or daughters start talking about their desire to go to the United States, many times causing heated family arguments. "I worry because when kids leave here, they are good kids. And when they return, if they return, many are drug addicts. They get mixed up with gangs. I told Juan [her son] not to go but he left anyway. Now it's been two months since I've heard from him. I wish he would call. When he doesn't call, I worry" (Putlecan woman, early forties).

Whereas Putlecan men and women differentiate Latin Americans by their nationalities and historical experiences, they categorize *los negros* (African Americans) and *los gringos* (white U.S. citizens) as comprising two separate homogeneous racial groups.[7] Putlecans describe los negros as *malos* (bad) and *peligrosos* (dangerous). Living in impoverished neighborhoods, often near large public-housing projects, the Putlecan migrants deduce "how African Americans are" from observing those they see hanging out or living on the streets and from news stories. The indigent, the alcoholic, and the criminal form the basis of their construction of African American identity, merging race with poverty. No Putlecans reported any interaction with middle class or wealthy African Americans. Even after I stated that in the United States there are many educated, wealthy African Americans, many Putlecans could not believe that they really existed.

Although few Putlecans' homes have actually been robbed in the United States, accounts circulate (and become more dramatic as they are told) in Putla from "eye-witnesses" who describe robberies by African American "gang" members.[8] These impressions of African Americans are based on superficial visual contact, hearsay, and fear that occur when language barriers and limited social interaction impede other types of communication that could counteract negative racial stereotypes. Moreover, most Putlecans I interviewed do not recognize African American historical experiences as being different from those of any other U.S. citizen. "I just don't understand why los negros are so poor and have so many *vicios* [vices]. They are legal and can get any job they want. We come without papers, find jobs, work hard, and progress. If we can do it, why can't they?" (Putlecan woman, early thirties).

While Putlecans divide norteamericanos into white and black racial categories, they focus on our shared legal status for employment opportunities, uninformed of the social histories of the two groups and especially ignorant of the discrimination African Americans have suffered. For most Putlecans who migrate for one purpose (to earn money), the United States is the "land of opportunity" once one can acquire work permits (either genuine or forged). In their minds, one is hindered in the United States only by one's legal status.

Whereas African Americans are stereotyped negatively, los gringos are described as *buena gente* (good people), *limpios* (clean), *sanos* (healthy), *educados* (educated), *civilizados* (civilized), and *progresistas* (progressive).[9] When I asked people how they know this, they explained how gringos "smile at you," "dress nice," "have big, modern homes," "work in clean jobs," "help other people," "know more than we do," "don't hit their kids," "are organized," "maintain everything is orderly," and "stop for firemen." One man remarked that while driving to work one day he almost had an accident because the car in front of him stopped suddenly for a rabbit in the road. He exclaimed, "Gringos even stop for animals in the road." These impressions stem from little intimate contact but rather from what people have seen or heard living in the new setting and from images on television. In urban areas, most Putlecans do not live in white neighborhoods.[10] Few Putlecans work directly with gringos or have gringos as their immediate bosses. Most of their supervisors are Latin Americans who are bilingual and serve as the intermediary between white owners or bosses and "Hispanic" laborers.

One Putlecan, a junior high school teacher, did speak negatively about white people. He said that at first he had the same positive impression of gringos that most Putlecans have. However after living in Chicago for a couple of years, he began to realize that many white people are prejudiced against Mexicans, but "because of their education, they know how to hide it better."

Housework is one of the few jobs in which Putlecan women deal with gringa bosses directly. However, because most do domestic work within a "job work" arrangement,[11] once the negotiation of the fee is settled, they only interact with their bosses occasionally. Most employers are outside the home working when Putlecan women perform the house-cleaning duties. The women who do this type of work have seldom expressed feelings of exploitation because they feel that they have more control over their time and a voice in the negotiation process.

> If I need more money, I can clean more houses. There's always more work. I am paid well. If I don't like how much she [the employer] offers, I just smile and shake my head no. Normally, she'll offer more. And often, the work is easy, just a little cleaning here and there. Dishes, laundry, all by machines, you know. You people [referring to my gringa-ness] are very clean so I guess that's why your houses aren't too dirty.
>
> (Putlecan woman, mid-thirties)

Not every Putlecan woman liked performing housework, but of those who complained, the majority had a live-in rather than a job work arrangement. Paid very little for their work and having no free time, these Putlecan women felt trapped and wanted to return home. One woman complained of having a boss who expected her to scrub all the floors of her "large" house every day besides completing all the other work. She stayed two months while searching for another job and for a place to live and then left when she found work in a factory and an apartment to share with three other women. She told me that though the factory job was also tedious and exploitative, she was free from the demands of that *loca* (crazy woman).

Owners of restaurants, pizza shops, and bakeries with whom Putlecans often have direct contact in New York City and in towns in New Jersey are often Italian Americans, whom Putlecans consider closer to "white" than Latin Americans but still more Latin than Anglo.[12] In part, this is due to their construction of Italian Americans as simply "Italians" and to the similarities of the Spanish and Italian languages. Owners give orders in Italian. Putlecans respond in Spanish, and *más o menos* (more or less) they understand each other. As one Putlecan told me, "at least it [Italian] doesn't sound as *extraño* [strange, foreign] as English." These workers discuss their exploitation by Italian American owners and are constantly shifting between restaurants and pizza shops for better pay. "You have to demand more money or *los italianos* will work you to death for nothing," a young Putlecan man who worked in three pizza shops in one summer told me.

When traveling in the United States, migrants were impressed by how "clean" the country is. In their interpretations, cleanliness resulted from education and a more "advanced" civilization.

> I had just arrived at my sister's in New Jersey. It was hot so I decided to get an ice cream. I came out of the store and threw the wrapper on the street, when this gringa picked it up and started telling me something in English. I don't know what she said, but I was embarrassed. I felt stupid. I never threw trash on the street again. You can't do that there. They're much more civilized than we are.
>
> (Putlecan woman, early forties)

Several Putlecans remarked on the difference between their neighborhoods, where people of color live, and the "rest" of the country. "There [U.S.] everything is clean and lots of trees and grass. Only where we lived with paisanos and los negros it was dirty. We don't know how to take care of things like los gringos do. No trash along the roads; the beach is very clean. I guess they're just more advanced. They're all educated" (Putlecan man, early twenties).[13]

Cleanliness and skin color are surface bodily traits. In an advanced capitalist society, the image of the body is manipulated to reproduce mainstream ideologies and middle-class values. In order for new immigrants to be "presentable," a multitude of consumer goods are offered to help them become "whiter."[14] As Putlecan migrants learn to re-present themselves in the new bicultural context (often by trying to distinguish themselves from some of their neighbors), one of the first things they buy are new clothes and *lociones* (perfumes, lotions, aftershave). In the United States, their new ways of cleansing and dressing their bodies allow them to feel more "modern" and as keeping up with the "style" of the middle-class gringos they emulate. Even though their income level may make them poor by U.S. standards, they use dress and bathing habits to create an illusory transcendence of class with the hope that they will succeed in achieving their desired economic gain and change the illusion into reality.

Rouse discusses how migrants in California are indirectly encouraged to adopt more U.S. styles in clothing, cars, and homes due to "disciplinary influences" of the INS and the police (1992:35). Most Putlecan migrants on the East Coast, however, view the police as helpful

rather than harmful, and their consumerism is driven from their negotiations of images and constructions of identities rather than pushed
by the fear of apprehension. This situation does not mean, however,
that Putlecans are completely free in their decision making. Social
institutions of the dominant society structure how these choices come
about and are defined in the first place.

Clothes and lociones are used by Putlecans in their hometown to differentiate themselves from Putlecans who have never migrated to the
United States, to make a statement about their success in the U.S. landscape, and to present themselves as persons who have become more
"modern" due to their migratory experience. They gain access to
resources that otherwise would be unavailable to them in Putla, and
they use these resources to imitate the actions of the wealthier Putlecans, who use clothing, cleanliness, and other material resources to display their economic potency. Through consumptive practices, many
migrants believe that they are now on par with those peers whom they
used to conceptualize as being "better." Few of their wealthier peers
agree, however. Buying power does not necessarily translate into social
power.

Migrants' constructions of the "other" (U.S. white and black citizens) do not begin afresh once their plane has landed in the new setting. These first impressions and living experiences reinvoke and
reinforce racial ideologies that have been handed down from generation to generation in their hometown. A Putlecan commented on
racism in the 1950s: "¡Cuantos detestan al gringo y quisieran parecerse a
él! ¡Cuantos dicen que no necesitamos inmigración europea y quisieran
casarse con una güera para 'mejorar la raza'! Nacionalismo a ultranza y
autodenigración, en boca del mismo individuo" (Ricardo Martell; cited
in Tibón [1961] 1984:158).[15]

In Putla, migrants grow up in a society where los indios and their
lifeways are routinely deprecated, where mestizos from more rural
communities are also called gente sin razón, and where people in the
wealthier classes describe Mexicans as a whole as "lazy" and sin cultura
(without culture). Everyday activities fuel racist ideas. For example, on
the weekends when indigenous people come to town to sell their produce, there are no public facilities for them to use. Thus, some wash
and many relieve themselves along the sides of houses in the center of

town. When they leave, waste is discarded around the kiosk. While they wait for buses, they are often denied access to restrooms, so they go in public spaces. They eat alongside the road, in a squatting position. I have heard young boys yell, "mira, los changos" (look, monkeys) and other disrespectful comments. Their lack of shoes and their dirty clothes, homes with dirt floors, and other scarcities of material resources nourish racist images and ideas.

In nationalistic events, such as the Independence Day parade, which are to supposed to glorify all ethnic groups, hierarchies are reinforced. In one 1993 parade float containing young women who represented "Mexico's plural society," the indigenous women, one Triqui, three Mixtecs, and one Amuzgo, were dressed in their native garb and placed around the feet of "Miss America" (a lighter-skinned mestiza) who rode in the center in a Western-style evening gown. However, although the society in which Putlecans grow up is racist, not everyone is a blatant racist. Many people from different classes believe that one should treat everyone with respect. Still, their beliefs about love for all humanity do not necessarily erase their other beliefs that rank people's superiority and inferiority by skin color. *Pobres inditos* (poor little Indians) may be a statement of empathy, but it also has an underlying sentiment of indigenous people as inferior. One Putlecan woman told me with great earnestness that "we need to help the Triquis because they're uncivilized. They would live like animals if we didn't teach them better." Her tone was not hateful but rather journalistic, one of reporting the "facts."

Hegemonic ideas, values, and attitudes about urban-Western lifeways fostered by public education and heightened by mass media images have shaped personal consciousness. The migration experience, in turn, supports homespun beliefs about class and racial hierarchies, that white people are wealthier because they are more educated and *más civilizados* (more civilized), for example.

Although most Putlecans construct los gringos in a positive manner, they are still aware of discriminatory practices in the United States. In their minds, the U.S. government is responsible for these practices. They separate *el pueblo* (the people) from *el gobierno* (the government) as they do in their own country.[16] It is in what Putlecans consider to be strictly family affairs that they resent the U.S. government the most. Several people repeated to me that if you hit your children, the U.S. government will come and take them away from you. Others also complained of government interference in child rearing. "Children need to learn to respect their parents. But there [United States] they don't have to because of the government. They can go and complain and the government will take them to live with a different family" (Putlecan man, mid-thirties).

A Putlecan woman in her late thirties stated, "I came home after my son was born. I couldn't take care of him and work enough to pay the rent and buy food and things. I was afraid to leave him with someone because the government would say that I'm not a good mother and would take him away." When I responded that many women work in the United States and leave their children in day care without any problems from the government, she rebutted, "Yes, they can. They're gringas. The government respects them."

Their disdain for the U.S. government also stems from what they see as its role in Mexico's economic calamities. The Tratado de Libre Comercio (TLC), North American Free Trade Agreement (NAFTA), is a current source of ill feelings. Although some Putlecans argue that it will be good for states in northern Mexico and others disagree, they all agree that it will be bad for the state of Oaxaca and its people. "Only for states that already have contacts, roads, and industry will the TLC be beneficial. Oaxacans will continue to migrate to be *la mano de obra* [laborers] like they are doing now" (Putlecan man, mid-twenties). "With the TLC, more companies will come and steal our resources like they're doing now—cutting down all our trees and now it doesn't rain like before. No, it's going to be bad for us" (Putlecan man, sixties). "It's like asking a cat and a mouse to play together. Sooner or later, the cat's going to eat the mouse" (Putlecan man, mid-forties).

The continuous news about NAFTA has intensified many townspeople's worries about the Mexican economy and their dislike for the U.S. government. By separating the U.S. people from the government, people see no contradiction in their conclusion that gringos are good and El Tío Sam (Uncle Sam) is bad. Uncle Sam discriminates against and oppresses Mexico and its people under its mighty economic and political strength. Several students and teachers in the COBAO and the Escuela Normal build upon these anti–U.S. government sentiments to push their students to continue studying and look for a professional job in Mexico rather than migrating "for fast money." "We have to keep our young people here. It's the only way Mexico will develop and progress," explained one teacher.

The migration process has reinforced hierarchies in the constructions of ethnic and racial identities for most Putlecan men and women. Although they may challenge the U.S. government, most often they accommodate and reinforce the ranking of people based on skin color in the new setting while renewing their hopes of becoming "whiter" by moving up the class ladder. In studies of immigrant settlement in the United States, researchers have shown that immigrant groups have resisted or reworked their placement within the ethnic and racial hierarchies of the dominant society, in part, by promoting ethnic pride.[17] Allegiance to the home country remains especially strong among first-generation immigrants, who recognize that they are "in America, but not of it" (Portes and Rumbaut 1990:140).

Time plays a critical role in influencing migrants' responses to these hierarchies. Putlecans who maintain relations in both their hometown and in the new setting but who see Putla as their home invest much less of themselves emotionally in the new place than do Putlecans who have settled permanently in the United States. Their loyalties are tied to Putla and to Mexico. As one Putlecan man told me when I asked about discrimination in the United States, "Who's got time to worry about these things? I'm here to work as much as I can so I get back home as soon as I can." The seasonal migrants' observations remain on a more superficial level. With time and increasing fluidity in the new social setting, these migrants may become more critical, as the junior high school teacher did, or they may remain unaware of or indifferent to the premises of their subordination in a place where they do not intend to stay.

Some nonmigrating Putlecans blame those who do migrate as "destroying" the Mexican family and community values. Despite their aversion to migrants who return boasting and showing off their new clothes or cars, their primary critique centers not on "U.S. imperialism" but rather on changing gender roles.

Gender Relations

Even though gringos as a "racial" group are perceived positively, for many Putlecans gringas represent a problem. Part of their construction of gringos as educated and advanced includes what they call "liberal attitudes," referring to equal rights for men and women. Many of the men and several of the women I interviewed resisted the idea of men and women sharing power, especially in the home.[18] Social life in Putla has been organized according to the principals of patriarchy—though with much variation among families as to how absolute.

Traditional patriarchal ideals, which relegate women to the private sphere in Mexico, have been changing in the past few decades as greater numbers of Mexican women actively participate in politics, wage work, and education.[19] Many younger people in Putla, especially those educated in a city, have begun accepting and supporting women's rights. But the ideology of machismo (manliness) is still strong in many families.[20]

Infidelity is construed as "men being men," and women are supposed to tolerate it. Many Putlecan men have had one legal wife and family along with one or more *casas chicas* (parallel families with lovers) throughout this century.[21] Women, on the other hand, are supposed to be virtuous and self-sacrificing for their families. When women step out of these bounds, they provoke severe criticisms from both men and women in the community, which often results in violent confrontations among their husbands, their lovers, and themselves.[22] Single women must be careful not to date too many men, or they risk being viewed as "used goods." "If she dates too many men, no one will want to marry her because, well you know [pauses]. You can't feel secure that she won't take off with some other guy later" (Putlecan man, mid-twenties).

Husbands' reputations hinge on their ability to control their wives and children, which for some men means physical abuse so "they know who's boss." One woman told me that her husband did not allow her to bathe until he came home in the evening. "He [her husband] thinks that if I bathe in the day that I must be fixing myself up to see another man or that I've been with him and am washing away the smell [of sex]. He's crazy" (Putlecan woman, late twenties). Control is exercised through control of women's bodies. Men who "lose" this control or those who do not adhere to what they consider old-fashioned ideas are the subject of jokes, even ridicule, about being *mandilones* (husbands who are ordered around by their wives).

For many men, part of their problem with gringas comes from their fear of losing control over "their women." Sharing power becomes emasculating. Many Putlecan female migrants have incorporated into their sense of identity "liberal" ideas of women's rights. For example, an unwed mother from Putla told me that before she migrated she was ashamed of having a child out of wedlock. She felt that people looked at her as if she were *sucia* (dirty, polluted), so she left Putla with her child to live with her cousin in Hoboken. While working to support herself and her child, she met several unwed mothers who felt no shame about having a child out of wedlock. After four years, she returned to Putla and opened her own tienda de abarrotes with the money she saved. She remarked, "Never again will I let someone treat me like a dog. I am a human being and I deserve respect. And now, can you believe that the father of my child wants to marry me? But I told him no. I don't need some drunken fool in my home."

Fathers, husbands, or brothers who resist "liberal" ideas and do not want their wives, sisters, or daughters exposed to them, manipulate the meaning of liberal to imply "antimother" and "whore." In their opinion, liberal women fail to follow the example of the Virgin Mary, who suffers silently for her family. The teachings of the Catholic Church are central in the lives of most Putlecan women. Men use this to keep "their women" in Putla when the women ask to go to the United States with them. They claim that they are "protecting their women" by keeping them away from "evil" influences, and in the process they defend their position of power in the family. Sadly, some men have even used the stories of two different Putlecan women who were murdered by their husbands while living in the United States as an example of what happens to a woman when she becomes too "liberal." Both of those women had separated from their husbands and were living on their own with their children.[23]

"Los hombres para trabajar y las mujeres para servir en el hogar" (men to work and women to serve in the home), as a young Putlecan man who continually denied his sister's request to go to the United States told me, "are the proper places for men and women." Not only in the home but in community events "proper" roles for women and men are expressed. During preparation for Independence Day celebration men strip pine needles and weave them together with ropes to decorate the municipal buildings and women serve trays of drinks and food to the men while they work. An elderly man told me, "this work is hard on the hands; that's why it's men's work." Women also serve food and drinks in all the neighborhood fiestas as well as in town festivals. In town parades, spaces are segregated by gender. For example, in the procession for the town's patron saint, La Virgen de la Natividad, women and children walk "protected" in the middle of the procession with the men encircling them on their horses. The image of men as guardians of the boundary between women and the outside world is reproduced.

"Mujeres para servir" applies not only in the home and in the plaza but also in the cantinas (bars), where women serve more than drinks (i.e., prostitution) and where men can articulate their machoness to the fullest. "The better man is the one who can drink more, defend himself best, have more sex relations, and have more sons borne by his wife" (Madsen 1973:22). The male drinking culture, which includes drinking *hasta atrás* (to drunkenness), having sex, and getting into fights, is one of the leading causes of conflict and tension in couples' relationships. An assertion of men's independence and authority, these actions hurt wives and children emotionally and financially, draining precious resources. Besides the money spent on alcohol and on women, fighting often results in a large debt. The fights get bloody and families have to pay off the injured party in order to have peace. Otherwise, the injured party seeks revenge and the fight escalates into a bloody feud between families.

Many Putlecan women are becoming less tolerant of macho ideals. Several women in their twenties told me that they have not married, because they do not want to spend their lives with *viciosos* (men given to vices). These women go out at night to restaurant-bars with their girlfriends to drink and to socialize, something they started doing while studying in Mexico City or Oaxaca City or while working in the United States. Many times they are joined by young couples. The younger men who prefer to go out with their wives rather than to the cantinas are chided by some of their male friends as having "wives who beat them."[24]

With the macho image under attack, some Putlecan men have begun actively denying that they are machos while often keeping macho ideals. Several men would preface their responses to my questions with "no soy macho pero . . ." (I'm not macho but . . .).[25] Although these men loathed physical abuse, calling men who hit their wives "animals," they still believed that a woman's place is in the home serving them and having babies. They naturalized their reasons, telling me, "that's how God made men and women" or "that's why women give birth and men don't." They conflated biological reproduction and social reproduction, concluding that child care is "naturally" women's responsibility. To defend their position further, they cited church doctrine.

Struggles over the meaning of gender and the rights and obligations of men and women have resulted in a loosening of social norms. Women exhibit greater freedoms. Men are increasingly participating in housework and in child care. Migration has played a central role in changing people's attitudes and behaviors, although there is much variation in migrants' responses at home and in the United States. When I first came to Putla, I was surprised to hear several women say that they were happy that their husbands and brothers migrated to the United States—not only because of the money but, more important, because of the changes in the men's behaviors. "He [her husband] came back [from the United States] much more respectful. Before he left, he was really *grosero* [uncouth], but now he's much more loving and helps me with the children" (Putlecan woman, late twenties). A teenager remarked about her brothers, "I didn't like being around my brothers sometimes. They were always saying *groserías* [vulgarities] and teasing me. But since they've returned from Atlanti [Atlantic City], they treat me well and they help Mom around the house. I couldn't believe it."

I wondered at the time if these were permanent behavioral changes or temporary actions because these men had missed their families. When I returned a couple years later, I visited these same women, who happily reported that their men were still respectful and continued to assist with housework and/or child care. As the husband of the Putlecan woman just quoted told me, "You never know what you have until you leave for a couple of years. My kids were babies when I left but not when I returned. I watched fathers with their kids in the park there [United States] and missed mine even more. You know, to love and *cuidar* [take care of] your children doesn't mean that you're not a man."

Almost half of the women in my survey responded that their husbands returned from the United States more respectful and responsible, harder working, and more cooperative with housework and child care. Several men had stopped drinking. The wives still performed the majority of household labor whether or not they also had income-earning jobs, but they did not mind because they feel grateful that God had given them "good men."

When Putlecan men migrate to urban centers in the United States and share an apartment, they have little choice but to cook, clean, and wash clothes for themselves. This experience causes many to change their attitudes about domestic work and to realize that housework is work. "I always thought that my wife just watched soap operas all day while doing a little cooking and washing. I never knew how hard it is to keep a house clean until I lived with a bunch of guys in Long Branch [New Jersey]" (Putlecan man, late twenties).

Even when couples migrate together, most husbands eventually learn to do housework. The majority of Putlecan women who migrate plan to work outside the home so that the couple can earn more money in a shorter period of time. Women complained to me of their double day in the United States. When couples first arrived, husbands expected their wives to continue taking care of the house (and the children, if they migrated with the parents) and cook as they did before, even though their wives were working full-time jobs. "I just couldn't do it all. I was exhausted and in a bad mood all the time. Finally I told him [her husband] that he had to help me. Thank God, he's a good man and understood. He started cooking dinner since he got home earlier than me" (Putlecan woman, early thirties).

Women's responses vary as to what extent men perform household tasks and to the degree of their consent. Some husbands were sympathetic and did what their wives asked, whereas others argued repeatedly with their wives over housework and reluctantly gave assistance. Several couples returned to Putla because these arguments were tearing apart their relationships. They felt that gender roles in the United States were too ambiguous. "It's easier here [Putla]. I work and my wife takes care of the house. It's not that I'm a macho; I love my wife and children very much. We decided together that it would be better to go back home. We earned enough [money] to set up my shop. We're much happier here because we know what each of us is supposed to do. We don't fight over housework and other things anymore" (Putlecan man, mid-thirties).

Migration to the United States does not automatically result in the creation of more balanced and better relations between men and women. To the contrary, migration can sever. I heard many stories of men abandoning their families in Putla once they arrived in the United States. For some, it was temporary: no communication or remittances for two, three, or five years, then the phone call announcing their return. But for others, the abandonment was permanent. Left to survive on their own or rely on extended kin, many wives of these migrants have become poorer and their children hungrier. As Stephen (1992) demonstrates, women shoulder most of the responsibility for the reproduction (childbearing and rearing) of labor power in Mexico due to the gendered division of labor. Migration is another process that can increase women's responsibilities and hardships even when husbands migrate but do not abandon them. For decades rural women have worked the fields and/or engaged in wage work while continuing with their own duties during husbands' absences (Crummet 1987; Simonelli 1986; Stephen 1991, 1992).

Some of my most difficult moments in Putla were when women asked me to find their husbands upon my return to the United States. Few women had addresses and of those who did, they were from several years ago. One abandoned wife told me how her husband boasted about having a new Chicana wife and then had the audacity to bring her to Putla for a visit. Furious, the wife tried to force her husband to pay child support (which she is entitled to under Mexican law) and to get the title to their agricultural lands for their sons. The husband paid off the police and the judge, paid no child support, and returned to the United States without signing over the lands.

About half of the women in my survey who had U.S.–destined husbands feared that their husbands would not return; the women worried that their husbands would get into accidents or become involved with other women. I heard of several cases of Putlecan men dying in car accidents in the United States, often because of driving under the influence of alcohol. Other women said that they were sure their husbands would return, "God willing," because they kept in contact and knew their husbands' plans. One woman explained, "He's always come home before. I know he will again." Another wife told me that her husband hated leaving Putla; he called her every two weeks even though it was expensive, because he missed her and their children terribly. A few women admitted that they felt no trepidation about their husbands' return because they did not care whether they came back or not. "When he's here [in Putla], he's never here [in the house] so why should I care if he returns or not?" (Putlecan woman, early twenties). Another young wife remarked, "If he returns, fine. If not, who cares? I've got more important things to do than worry about him."

Several women commented that the worst consequence of out-migration was what they saw as the rise of *madres solteras* (unwed mothers). As the feelings of the unwed mother who I discussed earlier highlight, women who have children out of wedlock are stigmatized. Women are not branded if they get pregnant before they are married, which is a common occurrence and the reason that many couples marry young. There may be some gossip, but because they have husbands they are not labeled as sucia, unlike the women who deliver their babies with no men there to claim responsibility.

Older women say that younger women are confused about what it means to be "liberal." As mothers, they worry when they hear their daughters talking about their rights with girlfriends: "whatever men can do so can we." They try to prevent them from going out drinking, having sexual relations, and ending up pregnant but often to no avail. For these mothers, young Putlecan migrants with cars have corrupted the town.

> These boys return for the winter in their new cars and the girls go crazy. They are so easily impressed and they think these boys have money. And that's all they care about—finding a boyfriend who has money, who can buy her little gifts. In the evening when its starts to get dark just walk around and look in the cars, you'll see them "doing it." They think that men are a way to *sobresalir* [get ahead]. But what happens, the boys go back to the United States and a couple of months later, the girls are pregnant and alone. The boys are far away and they don't care. Often boys run north as soon as they find out that their girlfriends are pregnant. They don't want a family; they just want sex.
>
> (Putlecan woman, late thirties)

Cars are replacing horses as the principal symbol of male virility in Putla. In the past, older people commented on how a young man would ride his horse *para robar una mujer* (in order to steal a women) with or without her consent. Parents constantly watched their daugh-

ters to prevent them from eloping or from being taken against their
will—a futile practice in many cases. Now parents watch out for young
men in cars.

Single young men repeatedly told me that their desire to go to the
United States stemmed to a large degree from their "need" to own a
car. They believed that if they stayed in Putla, they would never earn
enough money to purchase one. The young Putlecan migrants who
drive their cars around the town, do so for manly display—one can
easily walk from the edge to the center of town in minutes. For young
Putlecan men, cars are a symbol of economic well-being, sexual liber-
ty, freedom, and power. As Bayley notes in his study on automobiles
and images, "A fast car has reserves of power. The very suggestion of
power has in itself a strong erotic content. . . . The relationship
between sex and speed has been a powerful tool in [automobile] marketing in the U.S. and Europe" (Bayley 1986:7, 31). These images are
also remarketed in Mexico.

Madres solteras are not a new phenomena in Putla. I spoke with several older women who had never married and who had raised their
children on their own. They all agreed that it was very difficult especially "back then," but most believed they made the right choice or
made the best of the situation. Having sexual relations out of wedlock
is also not new. Although they may be "doing it" in cars today, couples
have always found places to have sex. Church documents do show,
however, that the average age at which women marry in the church is
rising. More younger, unmarried couples are using birth control and
thus do not have to marry in their teens as a result of pregnancy.

Increasing availability of birth control and the growing social
approval of its use are altering the lives of younger women. The Mexican government began a comprehensive family-planning program in
1974 in response to the rapidly growing population rate. To avoid direct
confrontation with the Catholic Church, the government constructed
the idea of family planning around the slogan "a small family lives better" (Riding 1985:225). Top priority was given to disseminating information to rural areas through a media campaign. As Simonelli notes, the
campaign extended to "Mexican-made *novelas* or soap operas in which
the heroine is usually depicted as a contraceptive user" (1986:163).

As one Putlecan in her fifties put it, for her generation family planning consisted of having "all [the children] that God sends." Women

under thirty-five years old invariably said that they wanted a small family. Many of these women already had two or three children and used birth control to avoid having more. Younger women without children agreed that to have two was best. They cited financial concerns as the primary reason.[26] "Women before had kids and more kids without thinking of how they were going to feed them. Not me. Two and no more" (Putlecan woman, late teens).

Parents feel obliged to provide more goods and more education for their children than they had. "We were poor and ever since I was a boy, my brother and I worked to help the family. We studied hard, too, so that when we grew up we could give our children all the toys and things we never had. I want my kids to be able to study and become professionals. We're only going to have one more child [they have one son]. It's the only way to live better" (Putlecan man, early thirties).

Younger women determined to have small families expressed the need to increase control over their bodies along with their pocketbooks. "All those kids and what happens. Your body is over. You look fifty when you're only thirty. Poor and fat. The only way to get ahead is to have one or two children, no more. Otherwise, your life is over" (Putlecan woman, early twenties).

After women start having children, most find themselves more confined to the home. They stop participating in activities that provide physical exercise, such as playing on local basketball and volleyball teams. Many Putlecan women gain weight with each pregnancy and feel they have lost control of their bodies, which decreases their self-esteem. Younger women are especially conscious of their physical appearance. Images on television and in magazines reproduce and reinforce urban-Western ideals of female beauty: thin, tall, light-colored (the whiter, the better), soft skin and hands, and shiny white teeth.[27] Fatness is associated with backwardness. Many women told me that gringas are more beautiful than they are because "gringas know how to take care of themselves" (i.e., they are better educated and more "modern").[28] U.S.–style aerobic classes are now offered in Putla. The image of the round Mexican mother who can cuddle all her children on her lap is under attack as women begin to internalize media images of the "ideal" woman.[29]

Several older women agree with their daughters' desires to maintain their figures and to give birth to only a few children. One woman told me that she would have liked to have had two or three children instead of nine. It would have made her relationship with her husband better.

> After you have a lot [of children], you start to lose the *cariño* [affection, love] between you and your husband. You have so many to care for, you don't have the energy to be as loving and attractive as before. And your husband doesn't devote the attention to the kids like you do, so he doesn't understand and begins to *buscar en otros lados* [look in other places for a lover]. If you have a couple [children], you can keep the cariño with your husband and live a better life.
>
> (Putlecan woman, mid-fifties)

Other older women believe that it is morally wrong to regulate pregnancy for any reason. They strictly adhere to the declarations of the Catholic Church, which bans the use of birth control.[30] In my interviews, many of these women blamed the "bad influences of the United States" or television for the greater acceptance of birth control.[31] One woman explained that this was why women in the United States are "weak." "They don't have all the children that God intended them to have. That's why they get pains in the stomach, breasts, and back. I don't have one pain, not one, because I have eleven [children]. Now God doesn't want me to have any more, but if he did, I would" (Putlecan woman, early sixties).

Her husband was convinced that in the United States, it was against the law to have more than two children. If you did, the government would come and take them away. His friend agreed and added, "The [U.S.] government is strict and controls your family. When our people go there, they come back different, more controlled. No more this and that, strict like there [United States]. They lose their passion for life" (Putlecan man, late sixties).

The cost of birth control impedes many poorer women from taking the pill or using other forms; these women are continuing to give birth to large families. Lack of finances is coupled with ignorance about birth control. Several poorer women remarked that they feared the pill because "it will make you sick" or "it will make you more manly." Only recently have two OB-GYN specialists set up practice in Putla. When the doctors first came, they offered Pap smears for free, thinking that women did not have the test because of financial constraints. But few women accepted for fear of the examination and town gossip. Many women worried that people would think something "dirty" was going on if they went to the male doctors and showed their genitalia. For these women, only when one was giving birth was it acceptable to "open your legs that way" because one had no choice.

Many younger women stated that they wanted smaller families so that they could have a career. They wanted to finish their education and not duplicate their mothers' situations, "always cooking and washing." They wanted to work, stopping only while their children were young. Once the children were in school, they planned to continue with their careers. They saw education and wage work as a way to enrich themselves and to gain personal as well as financial independence. Mothers who wanted to study and to have a career but were denied the opportunity by their fathers due to patriarchal ideas were supportive of their daughters' desires, as were many younger husbands of their wives'. Several young fathers who had lived in the United States commented that they enjoyed taking care of their children. Some had even renounced drinking so that they can spend more time and money on their families.

Traditional gender roles are undergoing modification in Putla, but the changes are not absolute. The most common wage work for women are teaching and commercial enterprises.[32] Both of these activities have a history of women's active participation and allow women to continue their duties as wives and mothers. Teaching and caring for children are an extension of "motherly" duties. The numerous tiendas de abarrotes and other stores that women run are located within the home sphere.[33]

Migration has increased women's participation and decision making in commercial activities. Starting with the contracting of Putlecan men for the Bracero Program in the 1940s, men began migrating out of the region for months at a time and women started gaining more control over family resources and deciding how to use those resources.[34] Putlecan women began managing family budgets—monies from local production and remittances from their men in the United States. As local agricultural production became less and less profitable due to changes in the national and world economies, commercial activities and migration assumed greater economic importance in the town. Remittances helped women set up small businesses, a process accompanied by an ideology of women being *más listas* (more astute) with money and better at bartering.[35] Putlecan women who run family businesses have become more assertive and share greater equality in the home. They also have greater prestige and mobility in the community.

The number of women participating in wage work is increasing in Putla as is the number throughout the country. Official figures estimate a 25 percent increase between 1975 and 1990 in the number of rural Mexican women performing wage work (Stephen 1992:79). Hard economic times in Mexico have pushed single and married women into much needed cash-generating activities. Several studies show that one of the results of this process is the enhancement of women's own sense of strength and competence (LeVine 1993; Mummert 1988; Peña 1981; Stephen 1992). Women who perform wage work have greater access to other activities that bolster their own sense of empowerment. Putlecan female teachers have shared information on women or family "self-help" programs offered in Oaxaca City. Female *comerciantes* (merchants) have served as presidents of the Putlecan market association. Other working women have joined the Comité de la Integración de la Mujer (a relatively new women's group that assists women in economic need, especially single mothers). Putlecan women have taken active roles in the local ecology group, church activities, and other community groups.

The changes that many Putlecan women (especially those born post-1960) are experiencing in the division of wage work, housework, and community work; in control over their bodies and minds; and in their relationships with husbands, children, and other family members are complex and often inconsistent. Increasing access to opportunities coupled with growing social approval of those opportunities enhance women's empowerment in the home and in the community. As other scholars have shown, migration often leads to greater gender equality in housework, in spatial mobility, and in family decision-making (Hondagneu-Sotelo 1992; Mummert 1988; Pedraza 1991). Patriarchal reins are loosening but not without resistance from both Putlecan men and women. A woman's self-identification is still firmly tied to her reproductive abilities. Motherhood and child rearing are eminently valued by men and women, as I quickly learned from Putlecan women who warned me to *apúrame* (hurry up) and have a child if I wanted to keep my husband. *Suegra-nuera* (mother-in-law–daughter-in-law) relations are often rocky as mothers baby their sons and criticize their sons' wives for asserting "liberal" ideas and for not following "traditional" gender roles. Several nueras complained to me about their suegras' constant disapproval of their cooking as not being "good enough" for their sons.

The transformations in gender relations vary among families. It is difficult to measure these changes because patriarchal authority in the family is, and has been, renegotiated on a day-by-day, year-by-year basis. However, the trend toward more egalitarian relations between men and women is strengthening in the community. The constructed meanings of self-identification as gendered beings are created, modified, and defended in response to migration experiences, daily struggles, ethnic and class relations, and religious beliefs.

Religious Beliefs

About 90 percent of Putlecans are Catholic and two-thirds of these go to church regularly. The Catholic Church's influence in the construction of personal consciousness is strong, as exemplified in the debate over birth control. However, official religious doctrine is mediated in the local context by particular priests. Their attitudes and interpretations of orthodoxy play a leading role in how community members negotiate religious beliefs with daily actions (Simonelli 1986:161).

The current priest in Putla is well liked. Unlike many of his predecessors, he has gained the respect of the townspeople through his bounteous community service that extends well beyond his sacerdotal functions. Since his arrival in 1990, he and the Equipo de Trabajo (restoration committee) have raised over $U.S.80,000 for the renovation of the dilapidated church. He preaches about ecological issues and is a leading figure in the ecology group in Putla. He has donated church space for the recycling center and has launched ecological movements in many other communities in his parish. When my husband organized the first conference on AIDS in Putla, the priest asked me for a copy of the information so that he can "advise the congregation better." Although unable to endorse the use of condoms as a means to regulate birth, he believes that they can be used "to protect lives." His more liberal interpretations of church orthodoxy provide enough ambiguity to help change attitudes about contraceptives, among other things, for many church members.[36] The townspeople, in response to his "good works," organized an enormous fiesta to celebrate his fifteen years of clerical service in March 1994.[37]

Putla has been described to me by community members as a "fiesta town"—a town in which life is organized by the cycle of festivals. "When one fiesta is over, you began planning for the next," remarked a Putlecan women who has often served as mayordomo. Most of the fiestas are in honor of neighborhood saints, town saints (Virgen de la Natividad), and national saints (Virgen de Guadalupe) and of other religious holidays, such as Christmas, Easter, Ash Wednesday, and the Day of the Dead. Only during the three summer months when the rains fall hard is the town quiet except for some bull riding and horse races.

Fiestas unite community members and renew feelings of social solidarity for people living in and outside the community. Participation in festivals through mayordomo service increases family honor and reflects people's sense of communal obligation. Even when living outside Putla, migrants send money for festivals in order to fulfill their obligations and maintain their status as members of the community.[38]

At the same time, however, festivals are a space in which Putlecans can demarcate their social position in the community through the display of material resources. During the week-long celebration in honor of the Virgen de Guadalupe, many women wear indigenous clothing to symbolize their "shared humbleness" with the Virgin Mary. Wealthier Putlecan women do not wear just any indigenous clothing, though. They buy elaborate, hand-sewn beaded blouses that Amuzgos from Ometepec, Guerrero, sell for the equivalent of U.S.$100 to $200 apiece. The blouses are stunning, and although they are "indigenous" they serve to underscore the economic status of the women wearing them and to differentiate them from "real" indigenous women.

Religious pilgrimages to the Basílica de Guadalupe in Mexico City and to the Virgen de Juquila near the Oaxacan coast are made by Putlecans annually. The apparition of saints continue to be witnessed in the town, their images left not only for townspeople but for everyone throughout the region to come see and to pray to. While we lived in Putla, the Virgin "appeared" on the wall of one of the taco restaurants, leaving a yellow stain that according to everyone "looks just like the Virgin." One year before, a saint "appeared" in the road to La Cureña (one of the neighborhoods in Putla), leaving his image on a rock. Putlecans who lived in this neighborhood and the priest held a procession and fiesta on the anniversary of his appearance and planned to do so every year. Many people told me that as economic times became more difficult, they were spending more (rather than less) on religious offerings in hopes that the "*Virgencita* will answer our prayers."

Other poorer community members have turned to evangelism in hopes of improving their life economically as well as spiritually.[39] The greatest concentration of evangelists are in the Campo de Aviación, the poorest neighborhood in Putla and the one with the highest concentration of "outsiders" (new arrivals to Putla). The evangelists from the United States give food and medicine to people who are interested in converting. They often serve food to their followers after Sunday services.[40] The leaders claim to have nothing against the Catholic Church. They are in Putla simply "to spread the word about Jesus Christ, our Lord and Savior." In the services I attended, nothing was said that could be considered a direct attack on the Catholicism. However, the literature I read that was produced and distributed by the Pentecostals attacked the worshiping of saints and their images.

Fewer than 5 percent of the people claimed to be *evangelistas* in my survey.[41] The evangelist migrants are unwanted by a majority of the townspeople, who see them as a *molestia* (nuisance) and are annoyed by their conversion attempts. The association of evangelists with recent immigrants (the "outsiders") in the Campo neighborhood reinforces the negative stereotype that many "authentic" Putlecans have about these people as "always causing trouble." But the overall presence of the evangelists in the community has yet to cause the type of conflicts seen in other areas in Mexico, such as in the state of Chiapas (Rosenbaum 1993:179–181; Tangeman 1995). The Catholic priest commented that he saw evangelistas at many Catholic religious festivals and that many were *compadres* (godparents) for Catholic family members. Conversions have caused heated family arguments in a few cases but not to the point of bloodshed or the breaking of family ties.

Several Putlecan men became Jehovah Witnesses while in the United States and have continued practicing their new faith upon their return to Putla. One of these men's wives reported that after seeing how her husband had changed (stopped drinking, spent time with the family) she decided to convert, also, so that "he wouldn't return to his old habits." Migrants, however, comprise only a few of the new evangelist members. Most members are people who have never left Oaxaca.

The gringos delivering the evangelist message are not perceived in the same light as gringos in the United States. Evangelism is not considered a more "modern" or more "advanced" form of religion. To the contrary, people find it constraining and oppressive. The denunciation of the saints, of their images, and of the religious festival cycle goes against people's senses of community and of time. Putlecans invest a substantial amount of their time and their personal trust in the Catholic Church. Religious beliefs are deeply ingrained in one's sense of identity. Moreover, I believe that due to the less conservative attitude of the local priest and his bountiful community service, the Catholic Church seems more accessible and responsive to changes in the community and to people's problems. Had he been unwavering in church orthodoxy and inactive in the community, people might have been more receptive to other religious ideas.

The evangelist advance in Putla still lacks continuity. Pastors from the United States come and go, with years passing in between their visits. Their churches have yet to grow strong roots, but as the economic crisis worsens who knows how many will convert out of desperation to find a solution to their hunger pains? Changing religions is one of the only options available to the poorest Putlecans because most have recently migrated to Putla in search of economic opportunities and do not have the resources to send a family member outside the region.

Health and Sexual Relations

A *New York Times* article (March 8, 1992) woke me up to one issue of migration and health with the headline "AIDS is following Mexican migrant workers back across the U.S. Border." The article discussed migrants from a small town in Michoacán who were returning home HIV-positive and infecting other community members. I had not put much thought into this very serious issue, even though Janes pointed out more than a decade ago that "migration is one of the major demographic processes affecting world populations today. However, knowledge of how social and cultural discontinuity affect health remains poorly developed" (1986:175).

The *Times* article struck home again one morning in Putla while I was reading the August 26, 1993, issue of *El Imparcial,* a Oaxacan newspaper. An article focused on 111 AIDS cases reported in the Central Valleys of Oaxaca. I asked some of my neighbors what they thought about the article, but they became "too busy" to discuss it. During the next few weeks, I found that many people resisted talking about the subject, even those whom I had come to know well. Some Putlecans spoke about AIDS in a whisper and blamed it on what they considered "indecent" sexual behaviors, such as male homosexuality or bestiality between "los negros and monkeys in Africa." They saw themselves as isolated from the disease, locating it in Mexico's two largest cities, in the United States, and in Africa.[42] Most AIDS cases reported in Mexico are in large urban areas and tourist resorts (H. Carrillo 1994:130). By 1989 the majority of Mexican people infected were "homosexual" and "bisexual" men,[43] and the growth rate of the disease has been highest among these groups (Bronfman, Camposortega, and Medina 1989).

Putlecans assign the disease to the "other" who lives in other places, like Guadalajara or Mexico City, where there are large gay communities and where foreign gay men visit. Many also believe that "you can tell by looking at someone" if he or she has the virus, even though it takes years for AIDS to manifest. While medical doctors in the town recognize the frightening effects these beliefs have, most of them have also contributed to people's misinformation with their own homophobia. One doctor said to me that "if we didn't have all these *jotos* (gay men) here, we wouldn't even have to worry about it."

Ignoring the disease or assigning it to some "other" has not prevented the spread of the virus into the community. A Putlecan chemist who does most of the medical laboratory analyses reported that during the summer months in 1993, 4 people out of 98 tested HIV-positive. Most of the people tested had been living in the United States and identified themselves as heterosexuals. I was shocked by the high percentage (almost 4 percent), and, worse, I was reminded by the chemist that only a few people get tested and that "those who know that they should [referring to those who have unprotected sex with multiple partners in the United States and in Mexico], are the last ones to walk into my office."

In Putla several gay men, on the other hand, who have taken the responsibility to be tested, are HIV-negative.[44] The gay men I spoke with had the most accurate information about the disease, and they stay informed through connections with gay organizations and friends in Mexico City.[45] Several of these men had lived in the New York City area and were very concerned about their HIV status.

New York City and Los Angeles are two of the seven cities with the highest number of AIDS cases reported, and current research indicates a high correlation between "seropositivity and geographical closeness to these high-risk areas" (Carrier 1989:132). Most Putlecan migrants spend time in these two cities as either their final destination point or when en route to the New Jersey coast or traveling up the West Coast. Seasonal migrants to the United States have become one of the primary concerns of AIDS officials in Mexico, who have detected "what appears to be a shift in regional patterns: the increase in the number of cases in large cities appears to be slowing down, while smaller cities and towns with fewer cases have increasingly higher rates" (H. Carrillo 1994:131). Migrants comprise one-third of the AIDS cases reported in the state of Michoacán (131). Officials fear that the disease is spreading even faster than predicted in the short-term projection models, due to circular migration between the United States and Mexico, and between cities and towns within the country (see Mohar 1992; Romieu et al. 1991).

Living in a high-risk area does not mean that one will contract the AIDS virus. One can become infected in any town or region and whether one is gay or straight. The problem lies in people's sexual practices. As Heise (1989:117) points out, the high prevalence of "bisexual" practices among Latin American men has increased the spread of AIDS among women and children in Haiti, Trinidad, Tobago, the Dominican Republic, and Honduras. "Health officials fear that other Latin American countries could follow Haiti's lead. In Brazil and Mexico, for example, bisexuals account for 23 percent of reported AIDS cases; in Ecuador, for 40 percent" (Heise 1989:117).

A man's sexuality in Mexico is not defined by who his partner is but rather by the role he plays in sexual relations. "Feminine males, generally believed to have a preference for playing only the receptive role in anal intercourse, are labeled 'homosexual' by Mexican people. . . . Masculine males, on the other hand, generally believed to be interested only in playing the insertive role in anal intercourse, are not stigmatized as 'homosexual' by Mexican people" (Carrier 1989:133, 134). Masculine males consider themselves strictly heterosexual, even though they participate in what Anglos would label as bisexual behavior, because they play the masculine role in intercourse with other men and with wives or girlfriends. Because they identify themselves as "not homosexual," many of them feel that they are not at risk for contracting the virus; in their minds, AIDS is a "gay disease." Lack of preventive measures results in the transmission of the virus across genders due to the sexual practices that accompany this attitude (138–139).

The denial of the possibility of contracting HIV is problematic in Putla as well as in the rest of Mexico.[46] In Putla, people do not want to discuss this possibility or even think about the disease. Most men resist using condoms because "it doesn't feel as good." Some fear, as one Putlecan stated, "that people will assume that I have it [AIDS] or something [another disease]." Condom use is associated with venereal diseases. As this same man pointed out, in a small town like Putla word passes quickly about who buys condoms in the pharmacy. Whether engaging in sex with gay men, prostitutes, or lovers in the United States or in Putla, most men refuse to use condoms. One young man told me secretly that he had unprotected sex with women during his stays in the United States, but he could not use a condom to protect his wife and future children when he returned because "she would know that I'm unfaithful there."

I spoke to a couple of prostitutes who were worried about contracting diseases, especially AIDS, but who could not force their clients to use condoms. The very suggestion could make the client think the prostitute already had a disease. As one prostitute told me, "If I ask, he'll go to someone else. What can I do? I have children to feed now. I can't worry about something that may happen years from now."

The backlash from the political Right against the government's safe sex campaigns has further hindered AIDS prevention efforts by promoting the idea that "good" people do not get AIDS, that only social degenerates do. The media campaign developed by CONSIDA (National Council of AIDS) has backed off from its promotion of condoms for protection, replacing it with a more ambiguous campaign of "parental responsibility" because of pressure exerted by the Catholic Church, by the National Action Party (PAN) and by Provida, the group that opposes family planning (H. Carrillo 1994:142–144). Although the promotion of marital fidelity and abstention from premarital sex are the two surest ways to stop the spread of the disease, they are completely out of touch with reality—especially in the case of Mexican migrants who typically migrate during their younger years, when they are more sexually active, have more cash, and have easy access to male or female sexual partners.

In 1988, Mexico officially reported 1,502 AIDS cases (Heise 1989:116). By January 1993, reported cases had risen to 12,540 (H. Carrillo 1994:130). The official reports are considered to be a fraction of the actual total number (1994:130). The campaign to increase knowledge about the disease worldwide has led only to marginal changes in sexual practices in Mexico (Heise 1989:123). In Putla, the only segment of the population responsive to the information has been some men who identify themselves as homosexual. The self-identification of one's sexuality plays a key role in people's responses to the AIDS epidemic.

I have no figures showing how many Putlecans are HIV-positive. Those who have the virus or who have an HIV-positive family member are too scared of the community's response to openly admit it. Fear has driven the disease underground, which in the end is only going to increase the infection rate. I heard only of one case in which a man stated that he had AIDS. He did so after getting drunk, and the men in the cantina quickly grabbed him and threw him out of the town, threatening that if he ever returned, they would shoot him on the spot. Similar stories of intolerance were reported in the *New York Times* article mentioned.

I worry that the virus is spreading rapidly in the town and throughout the district as a result of the high circular migration rate in the region and of people's attitudes and sexual practices. Moreover, because the presence of HIV magnifies existing epidemics by weakening immune systems of its hosts, other diseases will become more onerous.[47] In districts, such as Putla, where medical resources are minimal and access limited, curable diseases still kill thousands. The current circumstances—the ramifications of people's beliefs about AIDS, their current sexual practices, and the community's high circular migration rate—suggest to me that the town and its people are going to have to deal with a lamentable health situation in the not too far future.

Negotiating Identities

The variety of critical perspectives Putlecans have about their own sense of identities and their differential experiences in particular places and times reveal how identities are grounded in the nexus of unequal relationships of class, gender, ethnicity, and sexuality. Alliances and divisions are challenged, negotiated, and defended based on the heterogeneity and the multiplicity of individual subjectivities. While family and other social networks connect people across spaces, these networks are also re-created in new contexts as people's needs and desires change. Migration studies have tended to emphasize the positive aspects of social networks often to the neglect of the conflict and the contradictions they can produce in people's lives.

Racial hierarchies work to create false differences among peoples and to mask significant ones (Quintanales 1981). Putlecan constructions of "race" contribute to their own subordination and oppression within the hierarchies yet, at the same time, provide a space in which people can contest and renegotiate their social locations. Putlecans manipulate spaces through migration in order to challenge their current social positions. They can become more "modern" and maybe "whiter" from their experiences in Mexican cities or the United States, but they can leave these places when they grow tired of the foreignness of the new setting or the control over their time exerted by foreign bosses. Returning home, they struggle with differences in how they see themselves and how family and community members now see them.

Feminist scholarship has emphasized that families and the "household" are not homogenous sites of sharing and cooperation, though those activities do often transpire in the home. Gender hierarchies and other relations of domination are contextually expressed, contested, and defended in the home and in the community. Migration, religious beliefs, and forms of global communication have played active roles in these negotiations. What can be a source of liberation for one person, in turn, can be a source of conflict for another.

Social relations do not change in a unilinear manner. Identities, meanings, and practices are redefined and re-presented in a relational process on local, national, and global levels. The next chapter will examine the connections between the broader socioeconomic and political transformations within Mexico and the international community, and the constructions of identities, migration, and social changes in Putla.

6

Putla, the State, and the International Economy

The [world] crisis that was tipped off by sharp rises in oil prices in the middle of the 1970s and culminated in the debt crisis of Third World countries in the 1980s differs from that of the 1930s because of three major changes: (1) the growing integration of the world economy, (2) the shift from industrial production to financial capital as the principal basis for accumulation, and (3) the diminishing resources available for subsistence production throughout the world.

(Nash 1994:10)

The Mexican authorities have never attributed an agricultural recession to erroneous economic policy. Instead, they always blame the heavens; adverse climatic factors cause these crises, especially insufficient rains.

(Calva 1991:104)

S tanding on top of la Loma,[1] looking across the valley floor at the maze of rivers, I kept thinking about the statement a local agronomist had made: "Putla isn't productive, that's why we are poor." Yet I stood there staring at the lush tropical valley with its abundance of resources. Rivers, forests, and wide stretches of agricultural land lay in striking contrast to the dry, eroded lands of the Mixteca Alta. Putla, as well as the nation in general, has had good annual rainfall since the late 1970s (Calva 1991:104). During the mango season, mango trees droop from the weight of so many fruits hanging from their branches as do banana, sapote, and other tropical fruit trees throughout the municipio of Putla. Yet people are rapidly abandoning agrarian production, especially since the 1982 crisis began. Followed by falling coffee prices in the 1980s, Putlecans lost hope of being able to support themselves by farming.

Calva (1991:104) argues that the current agrarian crisis in Mexico is caused by three interrelated factors, none of which are environmental: the decline in internal demand for foods, the decline in profitability of agricultural investments, and the initiation of structural adjustment policies by the government, which have caused a sharp decline in public investments and in the agricultural sector's terms of trade. For medium- and small-scale farmers, survival of the crisis has depended on a reduction in consumption. Millions of rural and urban Mexicans, many of whom were already suffering from nutritional deficiencies, have had to further decrease their food consumption, resulting in a widespread national nutritional crisis (110–113).[2]

According to Mexican and U.S. government officials and to leaders of international financial institutions (IMF and World Bank), every year Mexico's economy is "healthier" and is on the road to recovery. But when is "the recovery" going to take place? The Mexican people have had to endure yet another major devaluation of the peso in December 1994, which cut their purchasing power in half. Most people with whom I spoke in January 1995 felt betrayed by the past president, Carlos Salinas, for telling them that the country's economic and political situations were improving. People are worried about the rapid increase in crime, about the desperation worn on so many faces. The situation made me wonder about peoples' ability to tolerate the drastic declines in their living standards, especially when so many were already suffering from chronic hunger. How long can they wait for the promised recovery?

If we compare the national economic situation in which Putla is situated with the goals and practices of Putlecans, an obvious contradiction emerges. People want to consume more, not less. People struggle daily for their children to have healthier and happier lives than they have had. They are tired of working harder only to receive less for their toil. I empathize with their frustrations. What is perplexing to me, however, is how people continue to live with the striking contradiction between their own everyday struggles to survive the never-ending crisis and the official discourses that continue to tout Mexico as one of the model countries in its progression up the neoliberal "economic ladder."[3]

Certainly, the current exodus of Mexican people from their country to the United States is a major response to this contradiction. But it is not the only one. Most people remain in their country. They continue to struggle to earn a living in their hometowns or move back and forth between two towns. Others migrate within and across regions and states. Peoples' decisions are dynamic and change through time. Yet few, if any, of the coping strategies people have devised attack the validity of the austerity program imposed by the government in accordance with international financial institutions' interests.[4] For the most part, their strategies represent personal "adjustments" to the austerity measures, to the program that has caused a deterioration not only of health and educational standards, but also in the overall quality of life, with increasing crime rates and pollution problems.[5] How bad does the situation have to become before people unite with the Zapatistas and demand social, economic, and political justice?[6]

Living in Putla when the revolution began in Chiapas in 1994, I became more intrigued by Putlecans' relationship to the Mexican state[7] and how the Mexican state actively defends, modifies, and re-creates its legitimacy so that it can maintain its authority.[8] Current migration patterns are a result of the draconian policies of debt collection that have produced a staggering net transfer of financial resources from Mexico to "first" world institutions and to other macroeconomic and political policies that fall under the rubric of development and modernization. However, peoples' responses to development processes are not determined solely by structural factors. They are continually negotiated in multiple arenas (local, regional, national, and international) in which relationships between political and nonpolitical power are played out. Examining these negotiations allows elucidation of some of the reasons that Putlecans, through their own practices and ideas, support the interests of the dominant social order in Mexico.

The PRI Government and International Financial Institutions

Mexico has been governed by a single political party, the PRI, for the past seventy-five years.[9] The party has experienced many periods in which its legitimacy has been questioned and fought, but through effective strategies of co-opting dissenters and of selectively repressing those unwilling to be bought, the party still controls the government, however tentatively (McCaughan 1993).

The PRI, though powerful, is only one facet of the Mexican state. Different interests (national industrialists, investors, technocrats, labor leaders, peasant organizations) have realigned forces in times of crisis and prosperity, resulting in complex and heterogeneous Mexican state formation processes. Before the initiation of the crisis in 1982, the ruling bloc was dominated by national industrialists' interests, but since then a breakdown in the traditional order has resulted in a realignment of economic and political power (McCaughan 1993:14). A shift in the relationship between forces yielded to transnational finance capital, especially U.S. based, increasing its power and control (A. Alvarez Bejar 1987:95). U.S. transnational corporations are major players in Mexican trade, accounting for more than 40 percent of manufactured exports (Unger 1991). The election of President de la Madrid in 1982 and his successor, Salinas de Gortari, in 1988, both advocates of neoliberal economic theories, ensured that state agents would serve the interests of foreign capital.[10]

The Bretton Woods institutions (IMF and World Bank) have assumed substantial power in directing economic policies of many "third" world countries, including Mexico. In order to receive loans, countries must accept their demands, which include the privatization of state enterprises and the "transfer of resources from production for internal consumption to export sales aimed at debt payment in currency that has international backing" (Nash 1994:11). These institutions insist that their structural adjustment policies are necessary steps in the longer road of economic development. They claim that the social costs will wane as the benefits of "sustainable" economic growth "trickle" down to all citizens. However, as many scholars have pointed out, these policies have not only failed to achieve their desired results; they have further deteriorated the living standards of most "third" world peoples.[11]

> The most obvious aspect of this failure—or success, depending on your point of view—is financial. Every single month, from the outset of the debt crisis in 1982 until the end of 1990, debtor countries in the South remitted to their creditors in the North an average $6.5 billion in interest payments alone. If payments of the principle are included, then debtor countries have paid creditors at a rate of almost $12.5 billion per month—as much as the entire Third World spends each month on health and education.
>
> (George 1994:29)

The implementation of structural adjustment policies in Mexico is mediated by the PRI government. The pursuit of the export-oriented economy has undermined the livelihoods of millions of citizens and has greatly weakened the PRI's image as the "party of the revolution."[12] Since the 1968 student movement, the party has faced an increasing crisis of legitimacy, and the 1982 rupture has exacerbated this "crisis of authority."[13] However, even with the loss of support of the popular classes and of some sectors of the bourgeoisie, the PRI continues to

wield substantial power and "the project of transnational capital artic-
ulated by the economic policies of the PRI remains dominant"
(McCaughan 1993:27).[14] Faced with the politicoeconomic crisis, the PRI
government, with the help of private capital, has reworked its nationalist rhetoric and practices in order to "establish a common discursive
framework that sets out central terms around which and in terms of
which contestation and struggle can occur. . . . This discursive framework operates not only in terms of words and signs but also necessarily involves a material social process; that is, concrete social relations
and the establishment of routines, rituals and institutions that 'work
in us'" (Joseph and Nugent 1994:20).

Through the "project of moral regulation," the Mexican ruling circle
seeks to unify what are in reality diverse experiences of groups within
the society.[15] The current crisis is constructed to appear as part of the
"normal" and "natural" process of development—a process that every
country must undergo if it wants to "evolve" into a "modern" nation.
The unilinear evolutionary perspective presents the process as if it
were following the "natural laws of progress."

Linking recurring themes of open-market economy, modernity, and
progress with "first" world countries who have democratic govern-
ments, an abundance of consumer goods, and higher living standards
works to justify the claim that neoliberal economic development policies are "good" for Mexico. The unstated assumption is that there is
only one evolutionary path for Mexico to follow in order to overcome
the crisis. Alternative development policies, such as the Partido Revolucionario Democrático's (PRD's) social democratic model of growth
or Goulet's (1983) pluralistic development model, which are set in the
domestic arena, are actively submerged by the state's discursive
framework, which centers the terms of discussion in the international
realm.[16] As Salinas stated while president, "We live in a world market.
It has risks but also new opportunities for countries like Mexico, who
are secure in themselves, their culture, and history, and thus can participate in the world market with confidence" (Salinas 1990:524). Or in
the words of his predecessor in 1984, when the crisis continued to
deteriorate living standards, "It is in this uncertain and dangerous
world that we Mexicans must move. These are times of storm and risk,
but of struggle and opportunities as well. . . . We are proceeding with
the realistic reordering of our economy. These changes are aimed at

rebuilding a firm foundation for sustained and efficient economic development within the framework of a more egalitarian society" (de la Madrid 1984:104).

The theme of equality is expressed repeatedly through the use of the pronoun *we* in official discourse: "We Mexicans," united as one nation, must battle the international "other"—the "uncertain and dangerous world," as de la Madrid called it. This theme negates the existence of differential access to opportunities, which are determined by one's class, gender, and ethnicity on local, regional, and national levels. It works to create the belief that all citizens are making sacrifices for the good of the nation.[17] The manipulation of social identity is key for the legitimation of the state's new agenda. As Corrigan and Sayer argue, "To define 'us' in national terms (as against class, or locality, or ethnic group, or gender, or religion, or any other terms in which social identity might be constructed and historical experience comprehended) has consequences. Such classification are means for a project of social integration which is also, inseparably, an active disintegration of other focuses of identity and conceptions of subjectivity" (1985:195). The Mexican state has created, and actively defends, a "myth of national integration"—the belief that everyone has equal access to economic and political resources, regardless of class status and ethnicity—in order to ensure the political and economic ascendancy of the state's interests at the expense of Mexico's marginalized populations (Vélez-Ibáñez 1983:194–196).

The Solidaridad Project

The re-creating of a national identity, expressed through the theme of equality, is underscored in a recent national project called Solidaridad (solidarity). To supposedly soften the blow of declining public services and investments, then-president Salinas initiated the Solidaridad program, which has functioned as a critical component in the government's attempt to regain popular consent.[18] The program's slogan, *unidos para progresar* (united for progress), emphasizes the "collective will" of the Mexican people to overcome the country's current economic and political problems. Based on the principle of self-help, individuals donate their time, labor, and money in order to obtain basic services, build recreational facilities, and receive financial credit or land titles. The government, in turn, promises to support and assist with these self-help efforts.

The program is a nationally defined project in which each individual has an important part to play. The program links ideas of unity, equality, and progress with the improvement of the material conditions of life. Its discourse strives to constitute new subject positions—changing an alienated people in a crisis into "progressive" citizen workers who are building a strong nation. The package has been sold to the Mexican public primarily through the mass media.[19]

In the numerous television advertisements for Solidaridad, the scenario always follows the pattern of changing something negative into something positive. In the commercial for a new health clinic built by Solidaridad, a boy is saved from a grave illness. His parents work in the clinic to pay for their child's medical bill, happily becoming new "medical assistants" in the process. In another ad, a grandmother loses her husband and is afraid that she may lose her home, too, but is saved by friends working under Solidaridad, who obtain her land title. She becomes a proud "landowner." A mother who wants to start a small business but does not know what to do with her children learns about a day-care center organized by women in her neighborhood through Solidaridad; she can now become an "entrepreneur." Individual success is coupled with the "traditional" value of honor. In each commercial, the people and Solidaridad are united by *la palabra* (one's word): *"la palabra se respeta"* (one's word is one's honor). One gains in an honorable manner, not by hurting anyone else.

A closer look at the program's targeted population reveals that the "we" who are going to provide labor and resources are the poorer, more marginalized sectors of the Mexican population. In none of the media campaigns are wealthier Mexicans depicted as part of the "unidos para progresar." The program's self-help philosophy is designed to keep resources in the hands of the dominant group; the subordinated peoples must use their own resources to "progress." The project's construction of a national identity, however, masks the country's unequal social relations.

Putlecans often spoke about Solidaridad. Many believed the program would help solve some of their economic problems. Under Solidaridad, numerous streets in the town were paved. Although critical of the costs for this service, most people were happy to have new concrete streets that lessened the amount of dust and dirt entering their homes.[20] Townspeople reiterated themes from the program's media campaign in general conversations. For example, one Putlecan said she would survive the crisis by "La unión de todas las personas y la solidaridad, de esta manera se establecerían soluciones para todos los problemas" (Everyone united and together—this is the way to finding solutions to all our problems).

In August 1993, the governor of Oaxaca arrived in the town of Putla to pledge support for Solidaridad projects in fourteen communities in the municipio. A total of 58,890 new pesos (less than U.S.$20,000 at the time) were allotted for the construction of bridges, schoolrooms, restrooms, roads, basketball courts, drainage systems, street paving, and water systems.[21] Putlecans were promised funds to finish the construction of a sports park on the edge of town.[22]

It had been many years since a governor or another high-ranking official had visited the region. The people felt honored by his visit, even though most considered themselves apolitical.[23] With government funds, they built a stage, decorated the plaza, and prepared food and drinks. Most wore their best clothes. Local bands played. People applauded the governor's words and chanted, "unidos para progresar" and other cheers. People commented on how they were not forgotten, how things were going to change. Some older Putlecans even recalled Lázaro Cárdenas's visit to the region some fifty years before. With all the pomp and circumstance that normally accompany government ceremonies, a feeling of unity and empowerment was created, absorbing even the small group of protestors who came with banners to denounce the governor's imposition of the PRI town president. The protestors told me that though they hated the PRI and all its officials, they believed that the Solidaridad program was a "good idea."

The Solidaridad project is an example of a practical and theoretical activity that disguises inherent problems in the new state's agenda by propagating itself "throughout society and creating a new form of national-popular will for some immense historical task," that is, overcoming the crisis (Hall 1988:55).[24] The emphasis on "progress" and "unity" inspired many Putlecans. The theme reached out to their sense of communal responsibility and civic duty and to their desire for more "modern" living standards. As a student said, "It's now in our hands. We can stay here or do something in order to progress." Furthermore, by associating self-help with democracy and equality, the government eludes its responsibility to provide basic services to all segments of the population and all regions within the nation. The self-help philosophy supports the mandate for less public spending by the Bretton Woods institutions.

Development as a "Civilizing" Process

I briefly discuss the Solidaridad program for two reasons. First, I believe that the program was effective in penetrating the population and regaining popular support for the PRI during the Salinas presidency. The program illustrates how one facet of the Mexican state (the government) must continually re-create its legitimacy in the face of opposition.[25] In its political project, the PRI managed to reconcile the interests of the "development" agenda with people's traditional values of community, honor, and loyalty to the nation.

Second, I believe that the recurring themes of the Solidaridad project highlight the importance of examining people's consumptive practices and their ideas about modernity and progress in order to understand how consent is constructed in the wider arena of social thought. If the Mexican state ruled only by imposing its dominant ideology on the entire population through manipulation or force, then this imposition would be easier to expose and thus to oust than it turns out to be in practice. The internal structures that form a social order are more complex. Meanings, values, and practices that come to be dominant and effective are in a continual process of renewal, re-creation, modification, and contention (R. Williams 1991).[26]

Most Putlecans now believe that commerce is the only viable economic option if you want to live in Putla. They want to sell more goods in order to increase their own consumption of national and international goods and to construct homes with more amenities. Continually exposed to higher living standards via migration, mass media sources, and public education, Putlecans believe that to have more material goods is to "progress" and to live a more "civilized" or "modern" life. These institutions coupled with migration experiences have created, reinforced, and elaborated ideas about modernity and progress that concur with the interests of the dominant social order.

Television programmers' main purpose is to convince viewers to buy consumer goods that are produced in national and international markets. Public education emphasizes individualism and competition rather than communalism and cooperation. Migration experiences not only expose Putlecans to different living standards, but allow them to experience firsthand homes with kitchen appliances, indoor plumbing, and "comfortable" furniture;[27] highways without potholes; and stores with endless variety. Advanced technologies, such as computers, FAX machines, and satellite dishes further integrate the local community with the nation-state and the international community.

By putting into practice the theory of consumerism (i.e., increasing consumption of goods is economically and socially desirable), Putlecans support the state's agenda of opening market doors to transnational capital interests and, at the same time, enhance their dependence on outside economic inputs. These processes bind Putlecans irrevocably to the national economy, itself bound to the international economy.

Increasing consumption is not simply a material process. It is intricately tied to processes of identity constructions, as highlighted by Mexican television advertisers who associate material goods with racial characteristics (e.g., the "whitening" power of consumption). Consumption is a critical factor in social differentiation and in definitions of the self.

The construction by Putlecans of a white identity and a brown-black identity dichotomy in which white is linked to positive qualities (wealthy, civilized, educated, clean) and brown-black, to negative ones (poor, uneducated, dangerous, dirty) parallels the constructed dichotomy between the white "first" world countries and the darker "third" world countries in neoliberal economic theories. Hence, the "logical" conclusion reached by many Putlecans is that white norteamericanos are wealthier and own more material goods because they are more "civilized" (more advanced on the evolutionary scale) than darker-skinned peoples. These racist dichotomies, which underlie the development discourses, justify the world hierarchy by naturalizing arguments about evolutionary selection and competitive fitness. Thus, Mexicans must endure their current living situation until the nation "matures" from its childlike or uncivilized state into a "civilized adult." Differences between "first" and "third" world countries are reduced to the simplicity of essences upon which dualist oppositions are built.[28] The development discourses reflect and obscure forms of domination.[29]

Living with Contradictions

Migration has played an important role in the legitimation of the dominant social order. It helps alleviate Mexico's unemployment problem. It provides people with the opportunity to accomplish their goals of consumerism and to re-create their social identities. People can migrate seasonally and continue to live in their hometowns, rather than being forced by economic necessity to leave permanently and join the urban sprawl of the Federal District.

Migration to the United States is also blamed for problems in the family and in the nation that have been created or exacerbated by the development agenda. In Putla, husbands and fathers complain of their wives' and daughters' increased mobility and participation in the workforce, where patriarchal ideals are challenged. Rather than trying to understand young peoples' rationales, parents and teachers name migration to the United States as the reason their children and students do not finish school. Young migrants who left school to go to the United States told me repeatedly that they saw no future in studying for a career in a country that lacked job opportunities. They saw the frustrations of other young Putlecan men and women who have studied professional careers, such as architecture or engineering, only to return to Putla to find no jobs. These young people have ended up working in their families' stores or migrating to the United States. As one young man pointed out, "Why waste all that time studying, when you're just going to go to the United States anyway."

Instead of viewing migration as a response to structural adjustment policies' having intensified the un- and underemployment problem in Mexico, people blame migrants for abandoning their families and for failing to help their country develop. The media reinforces this idea. "Television commercials sponsored by the government urge rural Mexicans to return to their native villages and not to seek work over the U.S. border because 'your country needs you.' The implied message is that the country can provide a decent livelihood for all its citizens" (Goulet 1983:63).

Although many Putlecans believe that migration is beneficial to individuals but detrimental to the community, their opinions are shaped contextually. For example, one young man who declared migrants to be "traitors" and thus was adamantly opposed to abandoning Putla left after receiving a phone call from his older brother, who asked him to join him in Long Branch, New Jersey. Less dramatic changes in people's opinions and actions occur frequently as daily life presents new experiences, meanings, and opportunities. Putlecans' mixed feelings toward migration are just one example of how Putlecans live with contradictory ideas and practices. They want the town and its people to "progress," yet they want things to be as they were in the past. They strive to increase prestige by buying more material goods yet disapprove of conspicuous consumption. They are critical of NAFTA, the formal treaty, but support more nebulous ideas about free markets and development. They build larger houses and pave roads yet worry about the rivers' falling water levels, which in part result from the uncontrolled extraction of sand and gravel from riverbeds for construction. They compete with neighbors in their local businesses but share resources in community fiestas. They blast music by national groups on their radios yet are disappointed at dances if chilenas are not played. They use birth control and identify themselves as devoted Catholics. Their full range of beliefs and practices at any one time includes what Raymond Williams (1977) calls "oppositional" or "alternative" forms as well as the dominant and effectual.

Putlecans negotiate ideas about "progress" and "modernity" with "traditional" ideas. At times, they do see through the state's ideological manipulations. For example, no one believed the "official" version of the Chiapas revolution proclaimed by the government via Televisa. But, for the most part, they consciously support the interests of the dominant order. The contradictions lived out by Putlecans in the context of the macrostructural policies of the state reveal that by their own actions and attitudes, they are participants. Putlecans are neither passive pawns nor revolutionaries. They think and act within the field of constructed possibilities, accommodating, modifying, or rejecting meanings and practices as their needs and perceptions change.

Forging a Social Consensus

The search for identity through consumerism is part of the larger processes of the globalization of consumption and the internationalization of advanced capitalism, which have strengthened the importance of transnational money markets and the global division of labor. If, as Salinas states, "we live in a world economy," then Putlecans' deci-

sions to move to places with better job opportunities, without attention to national borders, is a logical response. They are not "criminals"
as U.S. anti-immigration groups depict them; they are following the
new "rules" of the global economy. When many Putlecans first heard
the news about NAFTA, they were excited. They assumed that "open
borders" meant the free flow of both goods and people. Not that more
Putlecans would have rushed to the United States. It just "would have
made the trip easier," as a young Putlecan man told me. For them, it
does not seem a just situation that capital can move freely across borders but that the laborers who produce and consume the goods are
forced to sneak across the border in their arduous journeys to el norte.

Following World War II, the Mexican government moved sharply to
the right, marking the end of the agrarian revolution and the start of
the industrial one. Advanced capitalism has penetrated regions
unevenly, but the constructed ideologies of development and modernization have permeated most of Mexican society, forging a social con-
sensus. These ideologies, which praise the "modern" industrial sector
and portray the "traditional" agricultural sector as holding back the
nation, are part of a larger historical consciousness, extending back to
nineteenth-century nation-building processes.[30]

The export-oriented economy is the material manifestation of the
development construct that serves the state's interests. As an ideological representation of a specific mode of accumulation, the development agenda represents international financial institutions as Mexico's
"indispensable partner" in the global economy. It is a social process in
which the concepts of progress, modernity, and growth become internalized and "commonsensical." Constructions of social relations by
Putlecans, in turn, affirm the development discourse to be "true"—a
feedback process. Their everyday consumptive practices and beliefs
support the political project of the dominant social order.

As Mohanty has shown, "white capitalist patriarchies institute relations of rule based on a liberal citizenship model with its own forms of
knowledge and impersonal bureaucracies" (1991:21). Impersonal bureaucracies, such as international finance institutions, transnational capital,
and state agencies, present their economic models as objective, neutral,
and based on scientific facts. But as Pantojas-García points out, "to con-
fuse a model with reality is to leave out the social or real-world basis of

development options and to underestimate the role of political conflict in the adoption of particular policies to the detriment of others" (1990:1).

The Putlecan agronomist's comment about Putla's not being productive, thus poor, illustrates that Putlecans assume personal responsibility for economic problems in the region. Like the government they sometimes blame environmental factors; more often they blame their own "lack" of modernity and progressiveness. But through migration and education (in the broadest sense), they work to re-create their identities in accordance with the development agenda.

7

Transnational Migration and Social Identities

Perhaps the most we can do is remain skeptical of available repre-
sentations, while continuing to ask questions about what, and who,
is not being represented.

(Bottomley 1992:167)

*i*n this study, I have examined the relationships between migration and the constructions of social identities and of social relations within local, national, and international contexts in order
to illustrate how social change in a small western Oaxacan
community is a complex, multifaceted process. Through close scrutiny
of everyday activities, the heterogeneity and multiplicity of Putlecan
subjectivities and experiences have been highlighted. New experiences and information technologies have led to a redefining and re-
presenting of meanings and practices, which have had both negative
and positive impacts on individuals, families, and the community.

Putlecans have internalized their own subordination through hegemonic processes, reproducing the dominant social order, yet they frequently challenge their own particular locations within this social
order. Migration experiences and the globalization of communication
and consumption in advanced capitalism have played key roles in
these processes. The multiplicity of defining elements in the construction of a person's identity allows her or him to maintain contradictory
notions of self. Putlecans may emphasize one or more aspects of their
identity (e.g., their class position, gender, ethnicity, nationality, religion, or sexuality) and downplay others in response to the particular
circumstances in which they are situated.

Migration

Studies on migration have tended to prioritize the role of economic
factors in these processes, often to the neglect of other aspects that
constitute and shape peoples' practices and decisions. Economics certainly do play a prominent role in understanding migration patterns,
but we need to broaden our perceptions and our investigations to
include other social variables, such as gender, "race" and ethnicity, age,
family, sexuality, and religion, which also directly and indirectly affect
migration experiences and the changes these experiences bring. Peo-

ple's decisions about whether they should leave their community or remain at home are influenced by a multitude of economic, political, and social factors. In the case of Putlecans, changing gender relations, media constructions, racial ideologies, family networks, educational differences among and between generations, and economic needs all play important roles in shaping migration processes.

In my study, I have underscored the economic and social changes in Putlecan consumptive practices because consumption is a central component of migration experiences. What I have emphasized, however, is consumption as a social process, one that channels resources and draws the lines of social relationships. When migrants send remittances to their families, they are helping them economically but they are also maintaining and renewing their social relationships and their connections with their home communities.

After the completion of the road that connected Putla to the national road system, the consumption of urban-Western goods increased in most Putlecan homes. Fostered by the "modernizing" attitude spread by migrants, by public education, and by mass media and other new technologies, new ideas and assumptions have emerged in defining what a person or family must have in order to reach or to maintain a particular living standard. Putlecans have internalized these ideas and images. Race intersects with class to reinforce the messages. Putlecans mark white skin color as progressive, modern, and civilized, and black or brown as backward and inferior. Migration to the United States has strengthened racial and class ideologies constructed in the home community. Putlecans use material goods, such as clothing, cars, lociones, and so forth to imitate white, middle-class norteamericanos in the United States and to make statements at home about their success in the U.S. landscape—to project themselves as people who are more "modern" due to their migration experience and to thus increase their social prestige in the home community. Consumption is a critical factor in identity construction and social differentiation processes.

While Putlecans use migration as a way to challenge their own particular location within the social order, their everyday activities and beliefs, in turn, support and reproduce the dominant social order. Putla is, and has been, an important regional commercial center since pre-Hispanic times; only today commerce is assuming a greater role in the community's economic livelihood as agricultural production continues to wane. Continually exposed to higher living standards, Putlecans believe that to have more material goods is to "progress" and live a more "civilized" or "modern" life like "first" world peoples have: they place faith in the "whitening" power of consumption. These beliefs concur with the interests of the dominant social order. Putlecan consumptive practices support the state's agenda of opening market doors to transnational capital interests and at the same time enhance dependence on outside economic inputs. These processes bind Putlecans irrevocably to the national economy and to the Mexican state, which are themselves bound to the international economy.

While supporting the social order through their practices and beliefs, Putlecans do at times resist dominant ideologies. The ideology of individualism has not completely destroyed the spirit of communalism. Putlecans criticize community members who boast about money, who refuse to support community fiestas, or who fail to help out other community members in time of need. Migrants send money for community projects, such as the restoration of the church, and they serve as mayordomos. Putlecans negotiate ideas about progress and modernity with traditional ideas. Their range of beliefs and practices at one time includes oppositional, alternative, and dominant forms. They think and act within the field of constructed possibilities—accommodating, modifying, or rejecting meanings and practices as their needs and perceptions change.

The changes in gender relations in the community highlight this point. Putlecan women do not form a homogeneous group. Their differing social positions and diversity of experiences produce a range of responses to the current challenges to patriarchal authority in the family. The same is true for Putlecan men. Although the trend toward more egalitarian male-female relations is growing in the community, many Putlecan men and women still adhere to traditional norms and find the challenges threatening to themselves and their families. Some Putlecans agree with certain changes in attitudes and behaviors and reject others. The remarks of Putlecan women demonstrate that people define equality and their own subordination differently. The constructed meanings are continually renegotiated in response to migration experiences, daily struggles, religious beliefs, and other social relations.

Putla is a large, mestizo community whose population is continuing to increase despite its high out-migration rate. When I came to work in Putla, I knew that many people migrated out of the community, but only after I finished my survey did I realize how many people were recent immigrants to the town and saw Putla as a place of opportunities. We are beginning to witness some major changes in migration patterns as the result of transformations in regional, national, and international economies. The past trend of migration from rural communities to primate centers, such as to the Federal District in Mexico, is changing in Latin American countries (Portes 1989:16). People throughout Latin America, now realizing that opportunities are limited in primate centers, are migrating to smaller cities and regional towns. As the turn of the century approaches, we will find that many of the migration patterns that have extended from mid-century to the 1990s will no longer continue as people devise new strategies for accomplishing their goals. Putla provides a glimpse of some of these changes to come.

Migration and Borders

Migration is an age-old phenomenon, yet in the late twentieth century it has emerged in the forefront of political debates worldwide. People's fears and ideological stands that underlie most of these debates have resulted in the proliferation of racist attitudes toward migrants and immigrant populations, especially in "first" world countries. People worry that our nations are being "invaded" and overrun by poor, uneducated "third" world peoples to the point of mayhem and loss of control over our societies. The situation is constructed as a one-way street. We tend to forget that many of our citizens (businesspeople, retirees, evangelists, foreign diplomats, military servicemen and women, researchers, expatriates, and so on) also migrate to, remain in, and exert considerable influence on "third" world countries. For those of us with European ancestry, our ancestors migrated to "third" world lands centuries ago and stayed whether they were welcomed or not. Their migrations dramatically changed the lifeways of peoples around the globe. Yet today our reactions to migrants who enter our borders range from genuine concern about cultural separatism to malice and hostility toward the newcomers.[1]

In the United States, the backlash against immigrants crosses political lines, with both liberals and conservatives participating in the public outcry (Mills 1994). Undocumented migrants are blamed for lowering wages, increasing unemployment, draining public resources, causing divisions among minorities, threatening U.S. security, and escalating criminal activities, especially drug smuggling.[2] "Illegal aliens could, then, eventually become a hotbed of agitation and disaffection which might at some point challenge the harmony and unity of American society" (James 1991:104). The media has heightened public anxiety among Caucasians with articles such as "What Will the U.S. Be Like When Whites Are No Longer the Majority?" (*Time Magazine*, April 9, 1990; cited in Mahler 1995:6). Except for Native Americans, U.S. society is a nation of immigrants, yet this fear of our society fragmenting beyond repair weighs heavily in debates about immigration. Blaming the "other" for our domestic problems is the easy way out. After the tragedy of the Oklahoma bombing in 1995, we should realize that what threatens the peace and stability of any country, region, or town are the reproduction of racist and sexist stereotypes and the creation of new hatreds.

If we want to reduce the number of people crossing our borders, then we need to go beyond setting up "closed-door" immigration policies, which are and will continue to be futile. We need to recognize our role in the migration trend—and to show how our ideologies, consumptive practices, and immigration policies stimulate migration. For example, certain U.S. immigration policies encourage the "capital drain" and "brain drain" of "third" world nations by offering residency or citizenship to those who can invest a million dollars in the U.S. economy and to those who can improve the country's business or scientific capabilities.[3] The departure of people with capital or with higher education from "third" world nations hinders the development of these countries and further marginalizes their people in the global economy. In the case of Mexico, development ideologies and NAFTA will continue to uproot millions of people, sending them in search of work and security in places within and outside their national borders. As Rothstein notes,"If we truly want less Mexican immigration, persuading the Mexican government to slow its agricultural liberalization would be one approach. Failing that, we could underwrite targeted industrial policy in Mexico, which, in violation of free trade rules, would subsidize the development of small industries in rural areas where peasants are being displaced" (1994:62).

Negotiating Borders

The destructiveness wrought by racist ideologies and by fear of the "other" is in no way unique to the United States and other "first" world nations. As seen in this study, Putlecans also blame "outsiders" for conflict and problems in their town. They too draw boundaries to distinguish "authentic" Putlecans from newcomers, failing to recognize that their parents or grandparents migrated to and settled in Putla years ago. As the local economy worsens, resentments and frustrations are directed toward newcomers rather than toward the more distant national and international policymakers whose actions continue to marginalize their town, region, and state.

People negotiate constructed political, economic, and social borders of self-identification throughout their life cycle. I titled this study *Crossing Borders* in order to underscore that the boundaries we create are not fixed and closed but, rather, flexible and fluid. Putlecans develop and sustain multiple social relations as they cross political borders. They negotiate new forms of self-identification, as well as of identifying others, within a multinational context. Unfortunately, often the boundaries people draw to distinguish "us" from "them" are based on racial stereotypes, ignorance (especially of history), and fear of the "other." Identities are grounded in space and time, and they transform as time passes; as people move across spaces; and as local lifeways, national policies, and global conditions transform. People react by accommodating, challenging, and resisting these changes and constructions, and they produce new cultural forms that incorporate individual practices and wider relations of social experience at particular historical junctures. Further reflection is needed to understand how these new cultural forms continue to reproduce class, racial, and gender hierarchies in differing contexts and how with our studies, we can work to dismantle them.

Appendix
Questionnaire

#_____ **Barrio (neighborhood)** _____

La Familia (The Family):

1. ¿Cuántos años tiene? (How old are you?)
2. ¿Sexo? (Sex?)
3. ¿Casado/soltero/viudo? (Married/single/widowed?)
4. ¿Tiene niños? (Do you have children?)
5. ¿Cuántos? (How many?)
6. ¿De qué edades? (How old are they?)
7. ¿En qué trabaja? (What kind of work do you do?)
8. ¿Qué grado escolar tiene? (How many years of school have you completed?)
9. ¿Le gustó la escuela? (Did you like school?)
10. ¿Porqué? O porqué no? (Why or why not?)
11. ¿Su madre vive? (Is your mother living?)
12. ¿Su padre? (Your father?)
13. ¿Cuántos hermanos(as) tiene? (How many siblings do you have?)
14. ¿Cuántos años tienen y de qué sexo son? (How old are they and their sex?)
15. ¿Casados/solteros/viudos? (Married/single/widowed?)
16. ¿En qué trabajan? (What kind of work do they do?)
17. ¿Cuántos años fueron a la escuela? (How many years of school have they completed?)
18. ¿Dónde viven ahora? (Where do they live now?)
19. ¿Si viven en otras partes, cuánto tiempo hace que viven allá? (If they live somewhere else, how long have they been living there?)
20. ¿Porqué se fueron de la casa? (Why did they leave?)
21. ¿Regresarán a vivir acá? (Will they return to live here?)
22. ¿En qué trabaja (o trabajaba) su padre? (What does [did] your father do?)
23. ¿Tiene coche usted (o sus padres)? (Do you or your parents have a car?)

24. ¿En qué trabaja (o trabajaba) su madre? (What does [did] your mother do?)

25. ¿Alguien en la familia es comerciante? (Is someone in the family a merchant?)

26. ¿Qué vende? (What does he/she sell?)

27. ¿En dónde los vende: Putla? Oaxaca? D.F.? Otros lugares? (Where do they do the selling: Putla? Oaxaca? Mexico City? Other places?)

28. ¿Habla mucho con su familia? (Do you talk much with your family?)

29. ¿Habla mucho con sus vecinos? (Do you talk much with your neighbors?)

30. ¿Le gusta mirar la televisión? (Do you like to watch television?)

31. ¿Por cuántas horas cada día la mira? (How many hours a day do you watch it?)

32. ¿Cuál es su programa favorito? (What is your favorite program?)

33. ¿De qué se trata? (What is it about?)

34. ¿Mira las telenovelas? (Do you watch soap operas?)

35. ¿Piensa que la vida acá es como en las telenovelas? ¿O es más como en D.F.? O los Estados Unidos? (Do you think that life here is like life in soap operas? Or more like in Mexico City? Or the United States?)

36. ¿Tiene video? (Do you have a VCR?)

37. ¿Escucha la radio? (Do you listen to the radio?)

38. ¿Lee alguna revista? (Do you read magazines?)

39. ¿Cuál(es)? (Which one[s]?)

40. ¿Lee el periódico? (Do you read a newspaper?)

41. ¿Cuál(es)? (Which one[s]?)

42. ¿Cuáles son unas de sus mejores experiencias? (What are some of your best experiences?)

43. ¿De qué religión es usted? (What religion are you?)

44. ¿Va a la iglesia mucho? (Do you go to church often?)

45. ¿Va a las juntas políticas? (Do you go to political meetings?)

46. ¿Qué partido apoya? (What political party do you support?)

47. ¿Qué piensa sobre la situación política de aquí? (What do you think about the political situation here?)

48. ¿Cuáles son las cosas que le gustan del pueblo? (What do you like about the town?)

49. ¿Las que no le gustan? (Don't like?)

50. ¿Va a las fiestas en el pueblo? (Do you go to the local fiestas?)

51. ¿Cuáles son sus favoritas? (Which are your favorites?)

52. ¿Si usted tuviera mucho dinero, que haría con él en este pueblo? (If you had a lot of money, what would you do with it in this town?)

53. ¿Cree usted que alguien puede hacer algo para mejorar su vida acá? (Do you believe that someone can make his or her life better here?)

54. ¿Cómo? (How?)

55. ¿Tiene su propio terreno aquí? (Do you own land here?)

56. ¿Sus padres? (Your parents?)

La Emigración (Migration):

57. ¿Quién decide si alguien de la casa debe emigrar? (Who decides if someone must migrate?)

58. ¿Cómo decide a donde irá la persona a buscar trabajo? (How does a person decide where they will look for work?)

59. ¿Qué es lo más importante para decidir a donde irá la persona? (What is the most important factor in deciding where a person will go?)

60. ¿Dónde cree usted que es más facil o mejor para buscar trabajo: ¿acá? ¿en una ciudad grande como D.F.? ¿en otra parte de México? ¿en los Estados Unidos? (Where do you believe that it is easier or better to look for work: here? a big city like Mexico City? in the United States?)

61. ¿Porqué? (Why?)

62. ¿Conoce usted las familias que se han ido? (Do you know families that have left?)

La Emigración en México (Migration in Mexico):

63. ¿Ha ido usted o un miembro de la familia a buscar trabajo en alguna ciudad grande en México? (Have you or someone in your family searched for work in a big city in Mexico?)

64. ¿En qué año se fue? (In what year did you/he/she go?)

65. ¿A dónde? (To where?)

66. ¿Porqué? (Why?)

67. ¿Le consiguieron trabajo sus amigos o parientes? (Did friends or relatives find you/him/her a job?)

68. ¿De qué trabaja(ba)? (What kind of work do [did] you/he/she do?)

69. ¿Manda(ba) dinero a su casa acá? (Does [did] he/she/you send money to your house here?)

70. ¿En qué se gastó ese dinero? (How did you [or your family] spend the money?)

Para aquellos que tienen hermanos(as) en otras partes de México (For those with siblings in other cities in Mexico):

71. ¿Volvió al pueblo o vive allá todavía? (Did he or she return here or does he or she still live there?)

72. ¿Tiene mucho contacto con ellos? (Do you have much contact with them?)

73. ¿Cómo? (How?)

La Emigración a los Estados Unidos (Migration to the United States):

74. ¿Ha ido usted o un miembro de la familia a buscar trabajo en los Estados Unidos? (Have you or someone in your family searched for work in the United States?)

75. ¿En qué parte estuvo? (Where?)

76. ¿En qué año(s) se fue? (In what year did you/he/she go?)

77. ¿Cuánto tiempo estuvo allá? (How long were you/he/she there?)

78. ¿De qué trabaja(ba)? (What kind of work does [did] you/he/she do?)

79. ¿Cuánto gastó por el viaje? (How much was spent on the journey?)

80. ¿Cuántas gentes del pueblo fueron con usted o con el miembro de la familia? (How many people from Putla went with you or your family member?)

81. ¿Hubo amigos o parientes que le ayudaron? (Did friends or relatives help you/him/her?)

82. ¿Mandó dinero a su casa? (Did you/he/she send money to your house?)

83. ¿Cuánto? (How much?)

84. ¿Trajo dinero a su casa? (Did you/he/she bring money to your house?)

85. ¿Cuánto? (How much?)

86. ¿En qué usó el dinero? (How did you [or your family] spend the money?)

87. ¿Qué cosas trajo a su casa? (What things did you/he/she bring back?)

88. ¿Está (estuvo) en contacto con la familia cuando estuvo allá? (Is/are [was/were] he/she/you in contact with the family while away?)

89. ¿Cómo? (How?)

90. ¿Ha tenido malos resultados la emigración a los Estados Unidos? (Did you have any bad experiences while or because of migrating to the United States?)

91. ¿Cuáles? (What were they?)

92. ¿Porqué volvió a México? (Why did you/he/she return to Mexico?)

93. ¿Hubo conflictos al regresar con la familia o los amigos u otras personas? (Have you/he/she had any conflicts with family or friends or anyone else since returning?)

94. ¿Vale la pena ir a trabajar a los Estados Unidos? (Do you think that it is worthwhile to go to the United States?)

95. ¿Porqué? O porqué no? (Why or why not?)

96. ¿De qué manera cambió la vida de su familia el dinero que ganó allá? (How did your family's life change from the money earned there?)

97. ¿Qué aprendió acerca de los Estados Unidos mientras estaba allá? (What did you/he/she learn about the United States while living there?)

98. ¿Aprendió a hacer algo nuevo? (Did you/he/she learn to do something new?)

99. ¿Qué? (What?)

100. ¿Regresará a los Estados Unidos? (Will you/he/she return to the United States?)

101. ¿Porqué? O porqué no? (Why or why not?)

102. ¿Cree usted que la emigración a los Estados Unidos ha mejorado o empeorado el pueblo? (Do you think that migration to the United States has made the town better or worse off?)

103. ¿Cómo? (How?)

104. ¿Cómo se sintió cuando estuvo en los Estados Unidos? (How did you/he/she feel while living in the United States?)

105. ¿Con quién se juntaba allá? (Whom did you/he/she hang out with?)

106. ¿Fue a la iglesia? (Did you/he/she go to church?)

107. ¿Qué le gustó sobre los Estados Unidos? (What did you/he/she like about the United States?)

108. ¿Qué no le gustó? (Didn't like?)

109. ¿Sintió algún peligro? (Did you/he/she feel any dangers?)

110. ¿Con la policía? (With the police?)

111. ¿Con la migra? (With the INS?)

112. ¿Cuál cree que es la opinión del norteamericano en relación con el mexicano? (How do you think North Americans feel about Mexicans?)

113. ¿Regresaba al pueblo por algún día festivo o algún cumpleaño? (Did you/he/she return to Putla for any festival or birthday?)

114. ¿Qué hizo para divertirse al principio allá? (When you/he/she first got to the United States, what did you/he/she do for entertainment?)

115. ¿Y más tarde? (And later?)

116. ¿Qué opina sobre los hombres en los Estados Unidos? (What is your opinion about men in the United States?)

117. ¿Sobre las mujeres? (women?)

118. ¿Sobre los niños? (children?)

119. ¿Como hombre/mujer, siente que hay más oportunidades por los hombres/mujeres allá? (As a man/woman, do you think that there are more opportunities for men/women there?)

120. ¿Llevó su familia con usted? (Did your family go with you?)

121. ¿Siente que sus rutinas diarias cambiaron? (Do you feel like your daily routines changed?)

122. ¿Porqué? (Why?)

123. ¿Hubo cambios en como se vestió allá? (Did you change how you dressed there?)

124. ¿Otros cambios en como vivía? (Other changes in how you lived?)

125. ¿Invitaba otras personas que no son de la familia a su casa allá? (Did you invite people who aren't family members into your home there?)

126. ¿Porqué? O porqué no? (Why or why not?)

127. ¿Sus niños fueron a la escuela allá? (Did your children go to school there?)

128. ¿La esposa trabajaba afuera de la casa? (Did the wife work outside the home?)

129. ¿Porqué? O porqué no? (Why or why not?)

130. (Si la esposa no fue) ¿Piensa que su esposo había cambiado cuando regresó de los Estados Unidos? ([If the wife did not go] Do you think that your husband changed when he returned from the United States?)

131. ¿Cómo? (How?)

132. ¿Cuándo él no está acá, cómo se siente usted? (When he isn't here, how do you feel?)

133. ¿Tiene miedo que no va a regresar? (Are you afraid that he will not return?)

134. ¿Porqué? O porqué no? (Why or why not?)

Notes

Chapter 1

All the translations of Spanish quotes, with the exception of those from translated works (see the references), are my own.

1. See chapter four.

2. In Mexico, the term *chilango* refers to people from the Federal District who identify themselves as more progressive and advanced than provincial Mexicans. As a result, most provincial Mexicans dislike and resent chilangos. There are some regional variations in its usage, however. For example, see Alonso (1995: 68, 239 n.2).

3. See chapter five.

4. Atlantic City is one of the principal receiving areas for Putlecan migrants in the United States.

5. See chapter four.

6. For the town's history from pre-Hispanic times to today, see Grimes (1995).

7. Kearney (1986b) provides an excellent review of these perspectives. For neoclassical approaches, see Herrick (1965), Lee (1966), Lewis (1954), and Todaro (1976). For examples of the structural-historical approaches, see Cornelius (1988), Portes (1978), Portes and Borocz (1989), Sassen-Koob (1978, 1982), and Wood (1982). For migration and household studies, see Arizpe (1982), Dinerman (1978), Kemper (1977), Murillo (1979), Pessar (1982), Roberts (1981), Selby and Murphy (1982), and Wood (1981). For migrants' networks studies, see Kearney (1986a), and Mines (1981).

8. See, for example, Barrett (1988), Benería and Roldan (1987), Hartmann (1981), Rapp, Ross, and Bridenthal (1979), and Sacks (1979).

9. Many of these accusations continue to be repeated in political debates today.

10. See Portes and Rumbaut (1990) for counterviews.

11. See, for example, Anzaldúa (1987, 1990), de Lauretis (1986), di Leonardo (1991), Haraway (1989, 1991), hooks (1990, 1992), Minh-ha (1989, 1991), Mohanty, Russo, and Torres (1991), Moore (1988), Ong (1988), and West (1993).

12. Roseberry describes the dilemma anthropologists face when looking at the "Americanization" of Latin America as one of rejecting "the homogenizing stereotype without retreating into the equally stereotypic comfort of the distinctiveness of his or her [the anthropologist's] 'own people'" (1989:82).

13. In chapter 5, I examine how Putlecans negotiate their identities in the nexus of unequal class, "race," and gender relations.

14. An excellent study that looks at this important issue and reveals the contradictions in the lives of Salvadoran immigrants in Long Island, New York, is Mahler (1995).

15. For example, Wolf (1982) has shown that the construction of the categories *race* and *ethnicity* occurred during the development of capitalism.

16. For an examination of various studies focusing on how migration influences African and Latin American women's social positions, see Tienda and Booth (1991). See, also, Berlin (1985), Pessar (1985), and Ruiz and Tiano (1987).

Chapter 2

1. See Kearney (1991) for a discussion of transnationalism and migration.

2. This is the Spanish word for "roots," that is, the historical and cultural roots of Putla. For a more detailed history of the area, see Grimes (1995).

3. Ferias were grand fairs held every twenty days in which people exchanged goods, paid tributes, and worshiped the gods, especially the patron of merchants (Dahlgren de Jordán 1954:241, 248–249).

4. Cook and Borah (1968:32, 38) estimate that the population in the Mixteca Alta alone dropped from 700,000 people at contact time to 25,000 people a century and a half later.

5. Alcaldes mayores were Spanish officials in charge of regional political districts, the *alcaldías mayores.*

6. The *tianguis* is "a cyclical marketing organization in which a series of marketplaces operate on a rotating basis on separate days of the week and in different locales" (Cook and Diskin 1976:16).

7. The infamous story of Malintzin, a noble indigenous woman who was given to Cortés and forced to give birth to the new mestizo race, epitomizes the situation many native women had to endure. A number of Chicana feminist writers reveal how the story of Malintzin has been manipulated to reinforce gender hierarchies then as well as now. Malintzin became la Malinche, the traitor, Cortés's helper in the conquest, symbol of sexual weakness and interchangeability. Malintzin personifies women's openness to sexual exploitation—a belief that continues to mark women as "abusable matter, not just by men of another culture, but all cultures including the one that breeds us" (N. Alarcón 1981:184).

8. These liberal reforms were intimately tied to an emerging national capitalism inspired by European and American models.

9. During colonial times, the Spanish used the term *cacique,* adopted from the Arawakan term meaning native chief, to refer to a hereditary indigenous ruler. During the nineteenth century, the term evolved to mean local political boss.

10. The Triquis are Putla's indigenous neighbors to the north of the town.

11. For example, one of the científicos, Francisco Bulnes, asserted that Native Americans are a weaker race due to their diet: he claimed that wheat eaters (Europeans) are naturally superior due to the nutritional excellence of the grain; rice eaters (Orientals) are inferior because rice is inferior to wheat; and corn eaters (Native Americans) are the most inferior because corn lacks several essential nutrients (Stabb 1959:419).

Chapter 3

1. To protect the privacy of individual Putlecans, all first names used in the text are pseudonyms.

2. La Concepción is a neighboring community to the north of Putla.

3. An *ejido* is an agrarian collective set up under the agrarian land reform in the 1917 Mexican Constitution. The purpose of the reform was to return common lands to communities, although the use of such lands was not determined solely by community members but subject to regulation by a national bureaucracy, the Departamento de Asuntos Agrarios. In many cases, ejidos were formed out of haciendas, especially in central and northern Mexico, where no previous agrarian community had existed.

4. A *cargo* refers to an office in the civil-religious hierarchy.

5. Many Putlecans allege that this family has robbed and has killed competitors (and anyone else who has stood in their way) in order to monopolize control.

6. "Putla isolated and out of touch until a few years ago, can now be reached by a 70-minute flight. A jump of only 280 kilometers from the capital [Mexico City]; but in time, the distance is two centuries. Putla is a living example of eighteenth-century Mexico. . . . Only now it's Spanish descendants in alliance with mestizos who exploit the Indians."

7. The effects of this change are discussed in chapter 5.

8. Tequio is an obligatory system of community work. Families take turns helping to clean and repair public buildings and spaces, such as the cemetery, school, kiosk, and roads. Elite families today continue to hire poorer Putlecans to complete their obligations.

9. "It excels, in Putla, our lamentable superiority complex over the Indian. . . . Not only the wealthier mestizos but the poor ones as well."

10. Many Putlecans still hold this belief today. See chapter 5.

11. *Comadres* is the term used to mark the relationship between a mother and the women who are godmothers of her children.

Chapter 4

1. See Aguilar Medina (1979), Kearney (1986a), Méndez y Mercado (1985), Sanders (1975), and Stuart and Kearney (1981) for studies of out-migration from Mixtec communities.

2. In 1994, seventy-seven pickup trucks were registered with the office of transportation in Putla to legally transport people and goods in the municipio. The truck owners earn a living as full-time chauffeurs.

3. Marriage records from 1852 to 1944 in the Catholic Church's archives in Putla list couples' birthplaces (except for one book that recorded marriages from 1923 to 1931). Almost half of the men and women from Putla married a person from outside the district. In another 20 percent of marriages, both the wife and husband were born in communities other than Putla.

4. The idea that people make pacts with the devil to become wealthy is shared by other Oaxacan groups. For example, the Mixes place monetary transactions in a moral framework. They contrast "good" money, which is earned by hard work and in a relationship with nature, with "evil" money, which is made by "selling one's soul to the devil." "Money earned in harmful ways—such as selling land to outsiders, cheating, stealing, gambling, or charging exorbitant interest rates on loans—is likely to be seen as evil" (Greenberg 1994:71). See, also, Nash (1995:13, 14).

5. In the 1960s and 1970s, the district of Putla had a higher out-migration rate than coastal districts in Oaxaca yet had a lower rate than those in the Mixteca Alta (Aguilar Medina 1979).

6. Mexican immigrants worked throughout the Midwest and in industries in Chicago as early as the beginning of this century, but the majority were concentrated in southwestern agriculture (Hondagneu-Sotelo 1994:21).

7. During the Reagan administration, a sharp increase in the value of beach properties along the East Coast coupled with tax breaks for second-home buyers led many local families to sell their beach cottages and land to people who then tore down the old cottages in order to build large, expensive second homes. Summer-business owners who depended to a great extent on university students as a seasonal labor force, found themselves short of labor because many students could no longer find affordable housing on the beach and had to look elsewhere for summer jobs. Migrants from Mexico and other Latin American countries have begun supplying the seasonal labor shortage.

8. Atlantic City, the once-famous beach resort, became run down and crime ridden in the 1960s and 1970s. To revitalize the city and attract visitors, officials approved gambling, and large casinos and hotels were built along the boardwalk. Revitalization cleaned up and renewed oceanfront properties but left the rest of the city, where the working-class population lived, as it was.

9. See chapter 5.

10. The different perceptions of the same U.S. institutions suggest the need to look at the political economy of particular states within the United States and their histories of ethnic and race relations in order to understand the differential treatment of immigrants and the immigrants' responses and actions.

11. I discuss this point further in chapter 5 and examine how it affects the identity construction of Putlecans in the United States.

12. A few Putlecans reported receiving approximately $100 a year. The most in remittances a family reported totaled just over $9,000 in one year from their son; they used the money to finish building their large, three-story home. Most Putlecans send about $500 at a time, be it once, twice, or however many times a year.

13. Polanco is one of the wealthiest neighborhoods in Mexico City.

14. Kaiser and Dewey (1991) have noted in their research on Mexican migration and diet that wives economize expenditures during their husbands' absences by substituting processed foods for traditional foods; for example, they substitute pasta, which requires less fuel to cook than beans.

15. Many U.S.–destined migrants have teaching degrees, although they have never worked as teachers. The Escuela Normal is the only option for higher education in the town. Many students study teaching because their parents cannot afford to send them to a university in another city. The year-of-service requirement upon the completion of the teaching degree impedes some young people from teaching. Typically one gets sent to poor, isolated villages up in the *sierra* (mountains) for one's service. The thought of living in one of these communities depresses some students, so they opt for migration to the United States instead.

16. "To resolve these problems (poverty, ecological deterioration, democracy, the economy) is the assignment of Mexicans today. . . . Now is your time to live and to build, to change and to improve [the country]. This is your place in the history of Mexico."

17. Not until 1970 did the first *secondaria* (junior high school) open in Putla. Of the generation born in the 1960s and the 1970s, 90 percent have completed elementary school and 69 percent junior high school. Of the people born between 1930 and 1950, only 34 percent completed elementary school, although many more studied a year or two of elementary school. Less than 10 percent of this cohort received education beyond the elementary level, by attending schools in Puebla or Mexico City. All were from wealthier families.

18. A few students declare that Mexico needs to rid itself of Western influences, but they comprise a tiny minority. Most students in and out of the classroom ridicule indigenous people, especially the Triquis, for the way they talk and dress: "pinches indios, ni saben hablar" (stupid Indians don't know how to talk, i.e, speak Spanish). The proindigenous students glorify the native roots of Mexico in their romanticized version of preconquest Mexico—a "time of peace, prosperity and equality," as one student explained to me. They do not recognize that their sentiments reproduce part of the larger Mexican nation-building process that also extols Mexico's indigenous past but, at the same time, tries to "modernize" living indigenous peoples by eradicating their customs and languages.

19. In 1994, approximately 30 percent of families in Putla owned a vcr.

20. The town sometimes receives two channels, but both are owned by Televisa.

21. See Britton (1994:247) for readings discussing the international impact of mass media.

22. Television has become so pervasive in the district of Putla that even in communities that have no road access, no running water, or electricity, people own televisions and use car batteries to run them.

23. Douglas (1994:14–19) in her research on mass media in the United States illustrates this point. The U.S. media has bolstered the image of Americans as "rugged individuals" while, at the same time, fostering the idea of the American woman as passive and dependent. Is she the Bionic Woman or June Cleaver?

24. When the Chiapas revolution began in January 1994, 24 *Horas* news coverage was appalling. It tried to minimize the event and never discussed what the government troops were actually doing. All killing was blamed on the revolutionaries. In order to counter the "official" version, a schoolteacher from the Chiapas highlands made a videotape of the initial takeover by the revolutionaries and the first two weeks of the government's military response, which included the torturing and random killing of numerous Chiapan peasants. This videotape was sent to Mexico City, where friends added statements made by Salinas and 24 *Horas* commentators, to underscore the lies of the "official" version of events. The tape was copied and sent (via teachers and relatives) to communities throughout the nation. A Putlecan teacher received a copy about a week after it was made. I was amazed at the speed at which the grassroots network distributed the videos. It struck me just how far reaching new technology, such as video cameras, can be as "weapons of the weak" (Scott 1985), especially in exposing people in positions of power who think they are untouchable.

25. Chilena-style music and dance were brought to the region by merchants from Chile during colonial times (Castro Mantecón 1982:8).

26. "North American glass bottles: the most sanitary material, glass keeps products intact and fresh. . . . Furthermore, glass is recyclable. Compare and then consume [the product]. You will see that glass is the best option."

27. About a third of the people I interviewed expressed the same beliefs as this young man. Another third believe that the town has improved due to migration: new houses, more stores, more money circulating. A couple respondents did not know whether the town was better or worse off. The rest said that it was both: individual families' economic situations had improved, which was good for the town, but morals and traditional values were eroding.

28. During El Carnaval of 1992, a group of young men dressed up as U.S. Gulf War soldiers.

29. There seems to be greater pressure to send more money around Christmas time. Family members who have not heard from their kin in the United States during the entire year will typically receive money in December. Mother's Day (May 10) is also a time when more remittances are received.

30. A 660-square-meter lot with a small, abandoned adobe house in the center of town was for sale for 300,000 new pesos (U.S.$100,000) in 1994. Land prices in general become cheaper the farther one moves from the center of town, but even so lots on the edge of town measuring ten by twenty meters averaged 30,000 new pesos (U.S.$10,000). Several lot prices were greatly overpriced compared to other lots in the same barrio (neighborhood). Owners told me that they were not anxious to sell and would wait until "someone returned" with enough money to pay their price.

Chapter 5

1. They view themselves distinct from *gente sin razón*, a term applied to indigenous people or to recent arrivals in Putla. Almost all of the wealthier Putlecan families are descended from one or two foreign-born grandparents or great grandparents. Most have lighter skin color and consider themselves to be criollo rather than mestizo. For them, criollos have more European ancestry (which they emphasize) than mestizos do.

2. The wealthiest family in the town (family of the main coffee buyer discussed in chapter three) is the dominant wholesale distributor of beer, construction materials, and goods sold in the tiendas de abarrotes. The family accepts dollars for payments and exchanges them for pesos, paying a lower rate than the official exchange rate. The male head of the family has political contacts on the state level and ignores municipal laws, social customs, and anything else that prevents him from exploiting local resources as he wishes. Many of the townspeople say they despise him, reporting that not only does he never contribute to the community but that they believe he has had people killed who have tried to get in his way—and he will do so again. Some say, "He's the devil himself."

3. In my survey, 81 percent of the people reported that they were politically inactive; 10 percent stated that they were active sometimes. Sixty-eight percent supported no political party, 26 percent the PRI, 5 percent the PRD, and 1 percent the Partido Popular Socialista (PPS). Most people believed that there was no reason to participate because the political system was worthless and corrupt. I was told repeatedly that "justice" was reserved for the rich. A small group, Comité en Defensa de los Derechos Humanos de los Putlecos (Committee for the Defense of Putlecan Human Rights), was formed by a group of schoolteachers and other citizens several years ago to demand the people's rights to clean elections and to social justice. Unfortunately, their efforts have had little effect on the political and judicial systems in the town. Fighting and dissention engulfed the last municipal elections as has happened in most elections in the past. The person who most people believed won the town presidency was not allowed to take office. The PRI governor stepped in and named the new president for the town. "It was dirty politics as usual," explained a committee member.

4. Bourdieu's (1977) term *symbolic capital* refers specifically to the formation of class differences; I use the term in a broader sense to explore not only class but also the formation of gender and ethnic differences because all constitute the social field in which power relations are played out.

5. In her research on cultural identities, Oboler (1992) found that Latin Americans living in New York City also reject the uniform label Hispanic. See Alonso and Koreck (1993:110–112) for discussion of the development of the category Hispanic in U.S. cultural and political struggles. See, also, Shorris (1992:xv–xvii).

6. In her study of Salvadorans in Long Island, New York, Mahler (1995:94–97) found that members of this group also complain about their fellow country-men and countrywomen not giving assistance and not following the social norms of their home country.

7. *Los negros* and *los gringos* refer collectively to men and women, unless otherwise indicated. *Gringa* or *gringas* refer specifically to a white woman or women of U.S. origin.

8. Putlecan men who described the robbery events to me called the groups of young men *bandas* (gangs), but whether they were part of an organized gang or just a group of youths stealing is unclear. When I asked them privately for more details about the events, I also found it unclear whether they had actually witnessed the robberies or had heard about them from other people while living in the United States. Salvadorans in Long Island, New York, report-ed to Mahler (1995:229–232) accounts of African Americans attacking them and in general share the same views about African Americans as those held by Put-lecans.

9. When they say "progressive," they mean it in the sense of advancing, of gradual betterment—not in the political sense.

10. Several Putlecan families that have settled in the Atlantic City area talk about wanting to move up the class ladder by moving south to Ventor or Mar-gate City, where mainly white people live. These towns have well-kept houses and townhouses with manicured yards—quite a contrast to most of the run-down working-class neighborhoods of Atlantic City.

11. Romero (1987:205–216) distinguishes housework done on a live-in basis from "job work"—housework done on a weekly or biweekly basis, in exchange for a flat rate of pay. The domestic worker cleans several houses each week, negotiating separately with each employer for the pay rate. See also Hondag-neu-Sotelo (1994:152–153).

12. In the New York City area, most Putlecan migrants live and work in Hobo-ken.

13. The irony here, of course, is in the fact that it is due to the labor of circu-lar migrants, immigrants, and African Americans that much of the "rest" of the country stays clean.

14. As Ewen notes, "In this transition, the problem was invariably who one *was*. Who one could *become* was the solution. In the finding of solutions, the emerging consumer culture would gladly oblige" (1988:74; italics in original).

15. "How many detest the gringo yet want to look like him! How many say that we do not need European immigration yet want to marry a person with whiter skin in order to make the race better. Nationalism to the utmost and self-denigration, from the mouth of the same person."

16. Most Putlecan migrants are nationalistic. They love their country but dis-like their government—the PRI. As one Putlecan man told me while we were discussing what it means to be Mexican, "soy cien por ciento Mexicano pero eso no significa que soy priísta" (I'm 100 percent Mexican but that doesn't mean I support the PRI government).

17. See, for example, A. Alvarez Bejar (1987), Bottomley (1992), Calagione (1992), di Leonardo (1984), Glick Schiller, Basch, and Blanc-Szanton (1992), Oboler (1992), and Portes and Rumbaut (1990).

18. There were clear generational differences in people's attitudes toward equal rights. The majority of older male and female community members tended to be against equal rights, whereas the majority of younger men and women were in favor. Across generations, however, there were both proponents and opponents.

19. For women in politics, see T. Carrillo (1986, 1990). For wage work, see Arizpe (1977), de Oliveira (1990), Fernández-Kelly (1983), LeVine (1993), and Mummert (1988). For education in urban Mexico, see LeVine (1993:201–202). In Putla, the percentage of women attending school, especially past the elementary level, has increased over the past several decades. When the Escuela Normal first opened, men comprised the majority of students; during the past few years a shift in gender ratios has occurred, so women now constitute the majority.

20. Some scholars assert that machismo has become stereotyped as something negative and destructive, whereas originally it signified positive behaviors: responsibility, esteem, generosity, and loyalty (Mirande 1988). The meaning of the term varies among Putlecans. For some men, machismo is something to be proud of. For other men and women, it is associated with backwardness and should be eliminated. Still other people have a middle-of-the-road position, approving of certain macho behaviors and spurning others. None of the people with whom I spoke, however, associated machismo with esteem, generosity, or loyalty.

21. Lomnitz-Adler (1992:128) attributes the practice of polygyny in Mexico to "the proletarianization of the peasantry," in which men have lost much of their authority over their wives and children "and so seek the satisfactions of manhood in polygyny or other conventional signs of manliness." He suggests that this practice increases men's power by keeping the families in a constant tug-of-war for their husbands and fathers' affections and resources. In Putla, I talked with several women who live in this type of situation, but there are also many wives who have kicked their husbands out of the home for trying to play this game. Women's separation from their husbands for infidelity is not an entirely new phenomenon, although this practice has increased in the past two decades. Two women I spoke with chose to raise their families without their husbands once they discovered their husbands were having children with other women. The women were now both more than sixty-five years old.

22. See Greenberg (1989:208–209) for a discussion of machismo and family honor in Oaxaca.

23. In one of the two cases the Putlecan husband, after hearing that his wife was seeing someone else, stabbed her to death in front of their son.

24. Most of these younger men have also lived outside of the district of Putla, and their attitudes have changed as a result of their migratory experiences.

25. I knew that because I'm gringa (i.e., "liberal"), some Putlecan men told me what they thought I wanted to hear and others felt the need to defend their views on gender relations if they did not believe in equal rights. But I also heard denials of being macho in many discussions among friends.

26. As Simonelli concludes from her research in a small town in northern Mexico, "faced with economic crisis and the social consequences of modernization, women will elect to reduce fertility" (1986:172). Women confront the "daily task of matching assets to needs" and have "little difficulty visualizing the relationship between family size and dwindling resources" (171).

27. See, also, Alonso (1992) for a discussion on feminine beauty and "whiteness" in a rural Chihuahuan community.

28. Many young Putlecan women are becoming what Blea (1992:92) describes as "coconuts" in the Chicana community: women with brown skin and a white middle-class mentality.

29. See Ewen (1988) for a history of how the mania for thinness developed in the U.S. commercial landscape and the destructive effect this mania has had on women. The absurdity of this ideal lies in the simple recognition that "the insatiable passion for thinness is, at bottom, antagonistic to the body's natural need to be fed" (1988:180).

30. When Pope John Paul II visited Mexico in 1984, he repeated the Catholic Church's hard-line stance against all birth control, including natural methods "when used expressly to avoid conception" (Simonelli 1986:160).

31. Several men also criticized soap operas as being a bad influence on women, making them *más libres* ("loose," morally lax).

32. Here I am referring to legal or what is considered honorable wage work. Prostitution is also one of the most common types of employment for women in Putla, and drug (marijuana) production and smuggling is a growing income-earning activity for women as well as for men.

33. Elsewhere in Oaxaca, marketing is considered "women's work" and is not distinguished from other housework duties. See Chiñas (1976:173).

34. See, also, Arizpe and Botey (1987) and Stephen (1991) for examples of Mexican women in other rural areas performing what is considered men's work after their husbands migrate.

35. "The marketplace in particular has been a traditional workplace for Latin American women from pre-Columbian times to the present" (Yeager 1994:xv).

36. One day when I was walking with the priest, two older men approached him to say hello. As they talked, one man said, "We are bad sinners, no Padre?" The priest responded, "No, we are basically good, only sometimes we sin." This response highlights the priest's distance from hard-line Catholic doctrine, which teaches the answer contained in the old man's rhetorical question.

37. Women served chicken mole (a labor-intensive chicken dish with a pepper-cacao sauce), beans, rice, tortillas, and two eight-tier cakes to the entire community so that everyone could "break bread" together. The festival began

at 10 A.M. with Mass and continued with music and dancing until well into the night. People came from throughout his parish, and most people gave him gifts to show their gratitude.

38. See chapter 4.

39. Pentecostals are the largest evangelist group in Putla, numbering some thirty or forty active converts (i.e., those who attend services and try to convert others). The first Pentecostal came to Putla in the late seventies but left a few years later. The current pastor arrived in 1992. There are also *testigos* (Jehovah's Witnesses) in the town. Although testigos have been in the region throughout the past several decades, they have converted fewer people than have the Pentecostals. I refer to adherents of these two groups collectively as "evangelists," following the majority of Putlecans, who do not differentiate between the separate sects.

40. Often when I arrived at one of the homes of the recently converted, they wanted to know what I was going to give them. I would explain that I had nothing to give, that I was an anthropologist, not an evangelist. It didn't seem to matter, however, for some who still assumed that because I was gringa, I must be an *evangelista*. Their assumption was reinforced by my own actions because I often attended evangelist services to learn about the evangelists' impact on the community.

41. I believe that some very poor people may have responded that they are *evangelistas* in the hope that I was going to bring them food and medicine.

42. In his research on AIDS in the Yucatán, Wilson (1995) found that people there also perceive AIDS as a problem of other places, not of the Yucatán.

43. The terms *homosexuality, bisexuality,* and *heterosexuality* do not have the same meanings in Mexican culture as they have in Anglo culture. For Anglos, when two people of the same sex engage in sexual intercourse both are labeled homosexual; people who have sex with both sexes are called bisexuals. In Mexico, two same-sex people can engage in sexual relations but both are not necessarily labeled homosexual; nor are those who have sex with members of both sexes classified as "bisexual." Mexicans define a person's sexuality based on the role a person plays in sexual interactions, not based on the gender of one's partner. I discuss Mexican constructions of sexuality further in the text. See, also, Alonso and Koreck (1993) and Carrier (1989).

44. Most of the gay men went to CONSIDA (Mexico's National Council of AIDS) offices in Mexico City to be anonymously tested for fear they would face discrimination and hostility if tested in Putla. The test results were mailed to them in Putla but were in English. I became privy to this information when they asked me to translate the results. I have no idea why the results were in English except that it could have something to do with CONSIDA receiving its funding and resources from the World Health Organization and other international organizations.

45. In his research on AIDS in Mexico, Carrier notes that "From 1983 to date, gay liberation organizations have continued to be a major source of accurate information for bisexual and homosexual males interested in learning about

the transmission of AIDS through high risk sexual practices, and how changes in sexual behavior can minimize the risk of being infected by the AIDS virus" (1989:137).

46. Villagrán (1993) conducted a study of more than 3,000 Mexican university students who supposedly were more informed than most Mexicans about AIDS yet perceived the risk of infection as very low. Moreover, these students did not associate condom use with prevention. See, also, Wilson (1995).

47. For example, researchers have found a link between HIV and tuberculosis, which they believe is propagating deadly TB worldwide. This connection "is especially worrisome in the Third World, where poverty, overcrowding, and lack of access to treatment make tuberculosis more lethal than in the West" (Heise 1989:119).

Chapter 6

1. La Loma is a hill to the north of Putla.

2. The World Health Organization reported that the country's nutritional levels were severely repressed between 1983 and 1986, dropping dramatically from what they had been the decade before (*Excelsior,* Mexico City, May 11, 1987; cited in Calva 1991:113).

3. The "economic ladder" refers to Rostow's famous book (1960), which outlines the "stages of economic growth" through which countries must "progress" if they wish to join the ranks of "first" world countries.

4. The exception, of course, is the Zapatistas of Chiapas, who on January 1, 1994, began their revolution against the government in protest of their political-economic position in Mexican society and of their government's signing of NAFTA.

5. See Benería (1992) and Gledhill (1995) for an examination of the Mexican debt crisis and the social costs of structural adjustment policies.

6. The bold move by the Chiapans made Putlecans hopeful and excited yet, at the same time, apprehensive and worried. Most people agreed with the Zapatistas and waited anxiously to see how the government was going to react. The local priest and community members organized a collection of clothes and medicine to send to Chiapas. The town's president reacted by having a metal gate built across the entrance to his office. Identifying with the Zapatistas, people started feeling more empowered, and talk of change became widespread. Then in March 1994, a teacher was killed in Putleca, an incident also related to agrarian issues and government corruption. When the authorities failed to do anything about it, a mass demonstration was organized against the authorities' ineffectiveness and their corrupt practices. People of all ages, sexes, classes, and ethnicities marched to the town's plaza and demanded social justice. Banners proclaimed the people's support for the Zapatistas. Organizers remarked that the response had more participants and stronger emotional involvement than any previous demonstration. The town's president must have felt the same because he left town as quickly as possible. But

with time, emotions began to fade. People lost faith in the Zapatista movement, commenting that nothing would ever change in Mexico. People returned to gossiping about local events. Although many still wondered about "what could have been," most resigned themselves to the immediate tasks of daily survival.

7. I refer here to the state as a cultural form, not a thing (see Joseph and Nugent 1994:18–20).

8. I am following Corrigan and Sayer's (1985) argument on state formation, in which the "individualizing" dimension of state formation is emphasized. This dimension "is organized through impositional claims embodied in distinctive categories (e.g., citizen, taxpayer, head of household, *ejidatario*, and so on) that are structured along the axes of class, occupation, gender, age, ethnicity, and locality" (Joseph and Nugent 1994:20).

9. The party's original name was the Partido Revolucionario Mexicano (PRM). In 1946, the name was changed to the PRI.

10. The pursuit of foreign capital and the expansion of the export economy today mirror Díaz's attempts to "modernize" Mexico a century ago, resulting in many of the same calamitous effects (such as increasing malnutrition and debt, the loss of land and savings, and so forth) for the majority of the population, especially for those in rural areas like the region of Putla de Guerrero.

11. See Alvarez Bejar and Mendoza Pichardo (1993), Bello, Cunningham, and Ray (1994), Danaher (1994), Due and Gladwin (1991), Kidane and Logan (1995), and Ramsaran (1992) for critiques of structural adjustment policies that have been implemented in "third" world countries across the globe. See, also, Stein (1995:22, n. 2) for a partial list of the extensive literature criticizing structural adjustment in Africa.

12. From the late 1930s to the early 1970s, the PRI defined and created much of its legitimacy through a combination of revolutionary rhetoric, paternalism, corporatism, co-optation, some redistributive policies, and when needed, repression (McCaughan 1993:24).

13. Gramsci (1971) argues that effective and extensive forms of hegemony can emerge as the state arbitrates diverse interests but that these forms are transitory. Periods arise in which the masses "become detached from their traditional ideologies, and no longer believe what they used to believe previously," resulting in a "crisis of authority" (275, 276).

14. As Reding and Whalen point out, in order to ensure the party's position of power after the initiation of the crisis, the PRI has had to resort to a pattern of human rights abuses and state-sponsored violence. "Torture is universal, and dozens of journalists, more than one hundred members of political opposition parties, and a prominent human rights advocate have been murdered since Salinas took office" (1991:i).

15. Corrigan and Sayer define moral regulation as "a project of normalizing, rendering natural, taken for granted, in a word 'obvious,' what are in fact ontological and epistemological premises" (1985:4). A prime example of moral regulation is in their discussion of the "pervasive masculinity of the State" (12). By

regulating social identities of gender to clearly demarcate a new gender division in which women are relegated to a subordinate position throughout the capitalist world, the state parallels the patriarchal order of the family, rendering the domination part of the "natural" and "normal" processes of life.

16. For example, Goulet (1983) argues that Mexico needs a pluralistic development paradigm in which each policy is catered to a particular sector or a particular region, to meet the needs of the strikingly different regions that comprise Mexico. Not only should the strategies be pluralistic, but the planning and distribution of public resources must be decentralized in order to gain widespread popular participation. Both of his points are contrary to the neoliberal economic development paradigm pushed by the Bretton Woods institutions and enforced by the government. See Martínez (1990) for a discussion of the PRD's alternative economic program, which advocates the suspension of debt payments and the expansion of the domestic market and government spending.

17. As B. Williams demonstrates in her discussion of nationalism, "all bloods are not equal, but the precepts of nationalist ideologies demand that all subordinated groups bleed equally for the nation" (1989:436).

18. Long before his presidency, Salinas had been concerned about the investment in public works and how to use it to increase public support. In 1982, while director of the PRI party's Institute of Political, Economic and Social Studies, Salinas published a study comparing "the relationship between citizens' participation and the stability and survival of the political system" (the PRI) in Mexico (Salinas de Gortari 1982:30). He stated that his study arose from the need to change the ineffectualness of past PRI policy, which used spending in public projects to "buy the political support of groups which benefit from these projects" (3). He concluded from the study that a better way to increase public support was to increase participation of the beneficiaries in the implementation and administration of public projects. The Solidaridad program not only realizes this line of thought but takes it to its logical extreme—where "participation" means doing it yourself.

19. The systematic use of the media to support national development programs is not new in Mexico, nor in other "third" world countries (see Lent 1979).

20. One man objected to the high costs and he did not pay his share. When the street was paved, workers left the section in front of his house unpaved. Community members criticized him for being "cheap" and for failing to do "what is best for the town." The street project was also denounced by some of the ecology group members, who stated that paved streets were causing the daily temperature in the town to increase and that the concrete prevented the ground from soaking up needed rainwater.

21. If the funds were distributed evenly, each community would receive a little more than the equivalent of U.S.$1,000 for all these projects—a sum that was probably less than what the government spent for the governor's visit to the town that day. For a summary of his visit, see *El Imparcial* (Oaxaca City), August 17, 1993.

22. The sports park was to have soccer fields, basketball courts, a track, and a restroom building. The project was initiated in the early 1990s, but funds ran out before it could be completed. What was constructed is now overgrown with weeds.

23. See chapter 5, note 3.

24. Gramsci (1971) would call this phenomenon an "organic ideology." It "intervenes in the terrain of ordinary, contradictory, episodic common sense—to interrupt, renovate, and transform in a more systematic direction the practical consciousness of the masses" (Hall 1988:55).

25. The PRI suffered a decisive defeat in the 1988 national presidential election. Numbers were changed, however, and the winning candidate, Cuauhtémoc Cárdenas, of the PRD, was not permitted to take his seat.

26. As R. Williams (1991) notes, the construction of hegemony "is a whole body of practices and expectations; our assignments of energy, our ordinary understandings of the nature of man and of his world. It is a set of meanings and values which as they are experienced as practices appear as reciprocally confirming" (413).

27. While depicting what their life was like in the United States, Putlecans often described how "comfortable" furniture was there, because most Putlecans only had furniture made out of wood without cushions, pillows, and so on, and some still slept on petates.

28. As Minh-ha points out, dichotomies are used "as a tool of segregation, to exert power on the basis of racial and sexual essences, the apartheid type of difference" (1990:372).

29. One might wonder if there is no critique of such values in Putla. There is no significant organized political opposition in Putla (see chapter 5, note 3). Although Putlecans may critique the ways in which one displays one's "progress" (see chapter 4), the relationship between consumerism and "progress" is now deeply embedded in most Putlecans' minds.

30. The "traditional" agricultural sector refers to the growing of subsistence crops (corn, beans, chiles, and so forth), not export-crop production, such as coffee.

Chapter 7

1. Some people fear that the United States is losing its unity due to the entrance of foreigners, especially Spanish speakers, creating a country divided by linguistic and cultural barriers. English-only propositions, in part, stem from this disconcertment.

2. See, for example, James (1991) and Schlesinger (1992) for the advancement of this position. See Mills (1994) for counterarguments to the claims.

3. See U.S. House testimonies (1990).

References Cited

Archival Sources

AGN (Archivo General de la Nación), Mexico City.

1936   Sección: Lázaro Cárdenas, Ejidos, Oaxaca. 542.1/411.

1937   Sección: Lázaro Cárdenas, Ejidos, Oaxaca. 404.1/960.

AGEO (Archivo General del Estado de Oaxaca), Oaxaca City

1874   Legajo 67, Exp. 17, 6ff.

1888   Legajo 67, Exp. 19, 14ff.

1892   Legajo 67, Exp. 20, 19ff.

1908   Legajo 74, Exp. 7, 89ff.

Published Works

Adams, Richard

1975   *Energy and Structure: A Theory of Social Power.* Austin: University of Texas Press.

Aguilar Medina, José

1979   La Mixteca Oaxaqueña, una zona de emigración. In *Aspectos sociales de la migración en México.* Margarita Nolasco, ed., 155–185. Mexico City: Instituto Nacional de Antropología e Historia.

Alarcón, Norma

1981   Chicana's Feminist Literature: A Re-vision through Malintzin/or Malintzin: Putting Flesh Back on the Object. In *This Bridge Called My Back: Writings by Radical Women of Colors.* Cherríe Moraga and Gloria Anzaldúa, eds., 182–190. New York: Kitchen Table, Women of Color Press.

Alarcón, Rafael

1988   El proceso de nortenización: impacto de la migración internacional en Chavinda, Michoacán. In *Movimientos de población en el occidente de México.* Thomas Calvo and Gustavo López, eds., 337–353. Mexico City: El Colegio de Michoacán and Centre d'Études Mexicaines et Centramericaines.

Alonso, Ana

1992   Work and Gusto: Gender and Re-creation in a North Mexican Pueblo. In *Workers' Expression: Beyond Accommodation and Resistance.* John Calagione, Doris Francis, and Daniel Nugent, eds., 164–185. New York: State University of New York Press.

1995   *Thread of Blood: Colonialism, Revolution, and Gender on Mexico's Northern Frontier.* Tucson: University of Arizona Press.

Alonso, Ana, and M. Teresa Koreck

1993   Silences: "Hispanics," AIDS, and Sexual Practices. In *The Lesbian and Gay Studies Reader.* Henry Abelote, Michele Aina Barale, and David Halperin, eds., 110–126. New York: Routledge.

Alvarez, Robert R.

1987 *Familia: Migration and Adaptation in Baja and Alta California, 1800–1975.* Berkeley: University of California Press.

1994 Changing Ideology in a Transnational Market: *Chile* and *Chilenos* in Mexico and the U.S. *Human Organization* 53(3):255–262.

Alvarez Bejar, Alejandro

1987 *La crisis global del capitalismo en México, 1968–1985.* Mexico City: Ediciones Era.

Alvarez Bejar, Alejandro, and Gabriel Mendoza Pichardo

1993 Mexico 1988–1991: A Successful Economic Adjustment Program? *Latin American Perspectives* 20(3):32–45.

Anzaldúa, Gloria

1987 *Borderlands/La Frontera: The New Mestiza.* San Francisco: Aunt Lute.

Anzaldúa, Gloria, ed.

1990 *Making Face, Making Soul, Haciendo Caras: Creative and Critical Perspectives by Women of Color.* San Francisco: Aunt Lute.

Arellanes, Anselmo

1988 Del camarazo al cardenismo (1925–1933). In *Historia de la cuestión agraria mexicana, Estado de Oaxaca, 1925–1986.* Leticia Reina, ed., 23–126. Mexico City: Juan Pablos Editor, S.A.

Arizpe, Lourdes

1977 Women in the Informal Labor Sector: The Case of Mexico City. *Signs* 3:25–37.

1981 The Rural Exodus in Mexico and Mexican Migration to the United States. *International Migration Review* 15(4):626–649.

1982 Relay Migration and the Survival of the Peasant Household. In *Towards a Political Economy of Urbanization in Third World Countries.* Helen Safa, ed., 19–46. Dehli: Oxford University Press.

Arizpe, Lourdes, and Carlota Botey

1987 Mexican Agricultural Development Policy and Its Impact on Rural Women. In *Rural Women and State Policy: Feminist Perspectives on Latin American Agricultural Development.* Carmen Deere and Magdalena León de Leal, eds., 67–83. Boulder: Westview.

Bach, Robert, and Lisa Schraml

1982 Migration, Crisis, and Theoretical Conflict. *International Migration Review* 16 (2):320–341.

Barrett, Michele

1988 *Women's Oppression Today: The Marxist/Feminist Encounter.* London: Verso.

Bayley, Stephen

1986 *Sex, Drink and Fast Cars: The Creation and Consumption of Images.* London: Faber & Faber.

Bello, Walden, Shea Cunningham, and Bill Ray
1994 *Dark Victory: The United States, Structural Adjustment and Global Poverty.* London: Pluto.

Benería, Lourdes
1992 The Mexican Debt Crisis: Restructuring the Economy and the Household. In *Unequal Burden: Economic Crises, Persistent Poverty, and Women's Work.* Lourdes Benería and Shelley Feldman, eds., 83–104. Boulder: Westview.

Benería, Lourdes, and Martha Roldan
1987 *The Crossroads of Class and Gender: Industrial Homework, Subcontracting and Household Dynamics in Mexico City.* Chicago: University of Chicago Press.

Berlin, Maraglit
1985 Migrant Female Labor in the Venezuelan Garment Industry. In *Women and Change in Latin America,* June Nash and Helen Safa, eds., 260–272. South Hadley, Mass.: Bergin and Garvey.

Bernard, H. Russell
1988 *Research Methods in Cultural Anthropology.* Newbury Park, Calif.: Sage.

Berry, Charles
1981 *The Reform in Oaxaca, 1856–76: A Microhistory of the Liberal Revolution.* Lincoln: University of Nebraska Press.

Blea, Irene
1992 *La Chicana and the Intersection of Race, Class and Gender.* New York: Praeger.

Bottomley, Gillian
1992 *From Another Place: Migration and the Politics of Culture.* Cambridge: Cambridge University Press.

Bourdieu, Pierre
1977 *Outline of a Theory of Practice.* New York: Cambridge University Press.

Britton, John, ed.
1994 *Molding the Hearts and Minds: Education, Communications and Social Change in Latin America.* Wilmington, Del.: Scholarly Resources.

Bronfman, Mario, Sergio Camposortega, and Hortencia Medina
1989 La migración internacional y el SIDA: el caso de México y Estados Unidos. In *SIDA, ciencia y sociedad en México.* M. Bronfman, G. Ruiz, E. Stanislawski, and J. Valdespino, eds., 435–456. Mexico City: Secretaría de Salud, Fondo de Cultura Económica, S.A.

Bustamante, Jorge
1983a Mexican Migration: The Political Dynamic of Perceptions. In *U.S.–Mexico Relations: Economic and Social Aspects.* Clark Reynolds and Carlos Tello, eds. Stanford: Stanford University Press.
1983b The Mexicans Are Coming: From Ideology to Labor Relations. *International Migration Review* 17:323–341.

Calagione, John
1992   Working in Time: Music and Power on the Job in New York City. In *Workers' Expressions: Beyond Accommodation and Resistance.* John Calagione, Doris Francis, and Daniel Nugent, eds., 12–28. New York: State University of New York Press.

Calva, José Luis
1988   *Crisis agrícola y alimentaria en México 1982–1988.* Mexico City: Fontamara.

1991   The Agrarian Disaster in Mexico, 1982–89. In *Modernization and Stagnation: Latin American Agriculture into the 1990s.* Michael Twomey and Ann Helwege, eds., 101–119. Westport, Conn.: Greenwood.

Carmagnani, Marcello
1988   *El regreso de los dioses: el proceso de reconstitución de la identidad étnica en Oaxaca, siglos XVII y XVIII.* Mexico City: Fondo de Cultura Económica.

Carrier, J. M.
1989   Sexual Behavior and Spread of AIDS in Mexico. *Medical Anthropology* 10:129–142.

Carrillo, Héctor
1994   Another Crack in the Mirror: The Politics of AIDS Prevention in Mexico. *International Quarterly of Community Health Education* 14(2):129–152.

Carrillo, Teresa
1986   The Women's Movement and the Left in Mexico: The Presidential Candidacy of Doña Rosario Ibarra. In *Chicana Voices: Intersections of Class, Race and Gender.* Teresa Córdova, Norma Cantú, Gilberto Cárdenas, Juan García, and Christine Sierra, eds., 96–113. Austin: Center for Mexican American Studies, University of Texas.

1990   Women and Independent Unionism in the Garment Industry. In *Popular Movements and Political Change in Mexico.* Joe Foweraker and Ann Craig, eds., 213–233. Boulder: Lynne Rienner.

Castro Mantecón, Javier
1982   *Folklore de Oaxaca.* Mexico City: Imprenta Ajusco, S.A.

Chambers, Iain
1994   *Migrancy, Culture and Identity.* New York: Routledge.

Chiñas, Beverly
1976   Zapotec *Viajeras.* In *Markets in Oaxaca.* Scott Cook and Martin Diskin, eds., 169–188. Austin: University of Texas Press.

Chock, Phyllis Pease
1991   "Illegal Aliens" and "Opportunity": Myth-Making in Congressional Testimony. *American Ethnologist* 18(2):279–294.

Cook, Scott, and Martin Diskin
1976   The Peasant Market Economy of the Valley of Oaxaca in Analysis and History. In *Markets in Oaxaca.* Scott Cook and Martin Diskin, eds., 5–25. Austin: University of Texas Press.

Cook, Sherburne, and Woodrow Borah

1968   *The Population of the Mixteca Alta, 1520–1960.* Berkeley: University of California Press.

Cornelius, Wayne

1977   Illegal Migration to the United States: Recent Research Findings, Policy Implications and Research Priorities. Discussion paper C/77-11. Cambridge: Center for International Studies, Massachusetts Institute of Technology.

1978   *Mexican Migration to the United States: Causes, Consequences, and U.S. Responses.* Cambridge: Center for International Studies, Massachusetts Institute of Technology.

1988   The Role of Mexican Labor in the North American Economy of the 1990s. Paper presented at the Fourth Annual Emerging Issues Program for State Legislative Leaders: "The North American Economy in the 1990s." University of California at San Diego, La Jolla.

Corrigan, Philip

1990   *Social Forms/Human Capacities: Essays in Authority and Difference.* New York: Routledge.

Corrigan, Philip, and Derek Sayer

1985   *The Great Arch: English State Formation as Cultural Revolution.* Oxford: Basil Blackwell.

Crummet, María de los Angeles

1987   Rural Women and Migration in Latin America. *Rural Women and State Policy: Feminist Perspectives on Latin American Agricultural Development.* Carmen Diana Deere and Magdalena León de Leal, eds., 239–260. Boulder: Westview.

Dahlgren de Jordán, Barbro

1954   *La Mixteca: su cultura e historia prehispánicas.* Mexico City: Imprenta Universitaria.

Danaher, Kevin, ed.

1994   *Fifty Years Is Enough: The Case against the World Bank and the International Monetary Fund.* Boston: South End.

de la Madrid, Miguel

1984   Excerpts from de la Madrid's Second State of the Nation Address. *Business Mexico* 2(1):102–109.

de Lauretis, Teresa, ed.

1986   *Feminist Studies/Critical Studies.* Bloomington: Indiana University Press.

de Oliveira, Orlandina

1990   Empleo feminino en México en tiempos de recesión económica: tendencias recientes. In *Mujer y crisis: respuestas ante la recesión.* Neuma Aguiar, ed., 31–54. Caracas: Editorial Nueva Sociedad.

di Leonardo, Micaela
1984   *The Varieties of Ethnic Experience: Kinship, Class and Gender among California Italian-Americans.* Ithaca: Cornell University Press.
1991   *Gender at the Crossroads of Knowledge: Feminist Anthropology in the Postmodern Era.* Berkeley: University of California Press.

Dinerman, Ina
1978   Patterns of Adaptation among Households of U.S.–Bound Migrants from Michoacán, Mexico. *International Migration Review* 12:485–501.
1982   *Migrants and Stay-At-Homes: A Comparative Study of Rural Migration from Michoacán, México.* Monograph Series 5. La Jolla: Center for U.S.–Mexican Studies, University of California at San Diego.

Douglas, Mary, and Baron Isherwood
1979   *The World of Goods.* New York: Basic Books.

Douglas, Susan
1994   *Where the Girls Are: Growing up Female with the Mass Media.* New York: Random House.

Due, Jean, and Christina Gladwin
1991   Impacts of Structural Adjustment Programs on African Women Farmers and Female Headed Households. *American Agricultural Economics Association,* December, 1431–1439.

Durand, Jorge, and Douglas Massey
1992   Mexican Migration to the United States: A Critical Review. *Latin American Research Review* 27(2):3–42.

Esparza, Manuel
1988   Los proyectos de los liberales en Oaxaca. In *Historia de la cuestión agraria mexicana, Estado de Oaxaca, prehispánico–1924.* Leticia Reina, ed., 269–329. Mexico City: Juan Pablos Editor, S.A.
1991   Conflictos por límites de tierras, Oaxaca, siglo XIX. *Guías y Catálogos 7.* Oaxaca City: Archivo General del Estado de Oaxaca.

Etienne, Mona, and Eleanor Leacock
1980   Introduction. In *Women and Colonization: Anthropological Perspectives.* Mona Etienne and Eleanor Leacock, eds., 1–24. New York: Praeger.

Ewen, Stuart
1988   *All Consuming Images: The Politics of Style in Contemporary Culture.* New York: Basic Books.

Fernández-Kelly, María Patricia
1983   *For We Are Sold: I and My People.* Albany: State University of New York Press.

Flanet, Veronique
1977   *Viviré si Dios quiere: un estudio de la violencia en la Mixteca de la Costa.* Mexico City: Instituto Nacional Indigenista.

Foley, Michael

1995   Privatizing the Countryside: The Mexican Peasant Movement and Neo-liberal Reform. *Latin American Perspectives* 22(1):59–76.

García Alcaraz, Agustín

1973   *Tinujei: los triquis de Copala.* Mexico City: Comisión del Río Balsas.

George, Susan

1994   The Debt Boomerang. In *Fifty Years Is Enough: The Case against the World Bank and the International Monetary Fund.* Kevin Danaher, ed., 29–34. Boston: South End.

Gerhard, Peter

1993   *A Guide to the Historical Geography of New Spain,* rev. ed. Norman: University of Oklahoma Press.

Gledhill, John

1995   *Neoliberalism, Transnationalism and Rural Poverty: A Case Study of Michoacán, Mexico.* Boulder: Westview.

Glick Schiller, Nina, Linda Basch, and Cristina Blanc-Szanton

1992   Transnationalism: A New Analytic Framework for Understanding Migration. In *Towards a Transnational Perspective on Migration: Race, Class, Ethnicity and Nationalism Reconsidered.* Nina Glick Schiller, Linda Basch, and Cristina Blanc-Szanton, eds., 1–24. Annals of the New York Academy of Sciences, vol. 645. New York: New York Academy of Sciences.

Gmelch, George

1980   Return Migration. *Annual Review in Anthropology* 9:135–159.

Goldrich, Daniel, and David Carruthers

1992   Sustainable Development in Mexico? The International Politics of Crisis or Opportunity. *Latin American Perspectives* 19(1):97–122.

González Navarro, Moisés

1970   *Mestizaje* in Mexico during the National Period. In *Race and Class in Latin America.* Magnus Morner, ed., 145–169. New York: Columbia University Press.

Goulet, Denis

1983   *Mexico: Development Strategies for the Future.* Notre Dame, Ind.: University of Notre Dame Press.

Gramsci, Antonio

1971   *Selections from the Prison Notebooks.* Q. Hoare and G. Nowell-Smith, trans. and eds. London: Lawrence and Wishart.

Grasmuck, Sherri

1991   Bringing the Family Back In: Towards an Expanded Understanding of Women's Subordination in Latin America. Paper presented at the Sixteenth International Congress of the Latin American Studies Association, Washington, D.C., April 4–6.

Greenberg, James

1989 *Blood Ties: Life and Violence in Rural Mexico.* Tucson: University of Arizona Press.

1994 Capital, Ritual, and Boundaries of the Closed Corporate Community. In *Articulating Hidden Histories.* Rayna Rapp and Jane Schneider, eds., 67–81. Berkeley: University of California Press.

n.d. Caciques, Patronage, Factionalism and Variations among Local Forms of Capitalism. In *Descending the Pyramid? Mexican Political Culture.* Wil Pansters, ed. Wilmington, Del.: Scholarly Resources. Forthcoming.

Grimes, Kimberly

1995 Negotiating Borders: Social Relations, Migration Processes and Social Change in Oaxaca, Mexico. Ph.D. dissertation, Department of Anthropology, University of Arizona, Tucson.

Grindle, Merilee

1988 In *Search of Rural Development: Employment and Labor Migration in Mexico.* Ithaca: Cornell University Press.

Hall, Stuart

1988 The Toad in the Garden: Thatcherism among the Theorists. In *Marxism and the Interpretation of Culture.* Cary Nelson and Lawrence Grossberg, eds., 35–73. Urbana: University of Illinois Press.

Hamilton, Nora, and Norma Chinchilla

1991 Central American Migration: A Framework for Analysis. *Latin American Research Review* 26(1):75–110.

Haraway, Donna

1989 *Primate Visions: Gender, Race and Nature in the World of Modern Science.* New York: Routledge.

1991 *Simians, Cyborgs, and Women: The Reinvention of Nature.* New York: Routledge.

Hartmann, Heidi

1981 The Family as the Locus of Gender, Class, and Political Struggle: The example of Housework. *Signs* 6(3):366–394.

Heise, Lori

1989 Responding to AIDS. In *State of the World 1989.* Lester Brown, ed., 113–131. New York: W. W. Norton.

Herrick, B. H.

1965 *Urban Migration and Economic Development in Chile.* Cambridge: Massachusetts Institute of Technology Press.

Heyman, Josiah

1994 Changes in House Construction Materials in Border Mexico: Four Research Propositions about Commoditization. *Human Organization* 53(2):132–142.

Hondagneu-Sotelo, Pierrette

1992   Overcoming Patriarchal Constraints: The Reconstruction of Gender Relations among Mexican Immigrant Men and Women. *Gender and Society* 6(3):393–415.

1994   *Gendered Transitions: Mexican Experiences of Immigration.* Berkeley: University of California Press.

hooks, bell

1990   *Yearning: Race, Gender and Cultural Politics.* Boston: South End.

1992   *Black Looks: Race and Representation.* Boston: South End.

INEGI (Instituto Nacional de Estadística Geografía e Informática)

1950   *VII censo general de población, 1950, Estado de Oaxaca.* Mexico City: Secretaría de Industria y Comercio, Dirección General de Estadística.

1963   *VIII censo general de población, 1960, Estado de Oaxaca.* Mexico City: Secretaría de Industria y Comercio, Dirección General de Estadística.

1972   *IX censo general de población, 1970, Estado de Oaxaca.* Mexico City: Secretaría de Industria y Comercio, Delegación Federal de Estadística.

1984   *X censo general de población y vivienda, 1980.* Mexico City: Instituto Nacional de Estadística, Geografía e Informática.

1992   *Anuario estadístico del Estado de Oaxaca.* Aguascalientes: Instituto Nacional de Estadística, Geografía e Informática.

James, Daniel

1991   *Illegal Immigration: An Unfolding Crisis.* Lanham, Md.: University Press of America.

Janes, Craig

1986   Migration and Hypertension: An Ethnography of Disease Risk in an Urban Samoan Community. In *Anthropology and Epidemiology.* Craig Janes, Ron Stall, and Sandra Gifford, eds., 175–211. Norwell, Mass.: Reidel.

Joseph, Gilbert, and Daniel Nugent

1994   Popular Culture and State Formation in Revolutionary Mexico. In *Everyday Forms of State Formation: Revolution and the Negotiation of Rule in Modern Mexico.* Gilbert Joseph and Daniel Nugent, eds., Durham, N.C.: Duke University Press.

Kaiser, Lucia, and Kathryn Dewey

1991   Migration, Cash Cropping and Subsistence Agriculture: Relationships to Household Food Expenditures in Rural Mexico. *Social Science Medicine* 33(10):1113–1126.

Kearney, Michael

1986a Integration of the Mixteca and the Western U.S.–Mexico Region via Migratory Wage Labor. In *Regional Impacts of U.S.–Mexican Relations.* Ina Rosenthal-Urey, ed., 71–102. Monograph Series no. 16. La Jolla: Center for U.S.–Mexican Studies, University of California at San Diego.

1986b From the Invisible Hand to Visible Feet: Anthropological Studies of Migration and Development. *Annual Review of Anthropology* 15:331–361.

1991   Borders and Boundaries of State and Self at the End of Empire. *Journal of Historical Sociology* 4(1):52–74.

Kemper, Robert

1977   *Migration and Adaptation: Tzintzuntzan Peasants in Mexico City.* Beverly Hills, Calif.: Sage.

Kidane Mengisteab, and Bernard Ikubolajen Logan, eds.,

1995   *Beyond Economic Liberalization in Africa: Structural Adjustment and the Alternatives.* London: Zed.

Knight, Alan

1990   Racism, Revolution, and *Indigenismo:* Mexico, 1910–1940. In *The Idea of Race in Latin America, 1870–1940.* Richard Graham, ed., 71–113. Austin: University of Texas Press.

Lacy, Elaine

1994   Autonomy versus Foreign Influence: Mexican Education Policy and UNESCO. In *Molding the Hearts and Minds: Education, Communications and Social Change in Latin America.* John Britton, ed., 233–240. Wilmington, Del.: Scholarly Resources.

Lamphere, Louise

1992   Introduction: The Shaping of Diversity. In *Structuring Diversity: Ethnographic Perspectives on the New Immigration.* Louise Lamphere, ed., 1–34. Chicago: University of Chicago Press.

Lavrin, Asunción

1985   Investigación sobre la mujer de la colonia en México: siglos XVII y XVIII. In *Las mujeres latino-americanas: perspectivas históricas.* Asunción Lavrin, ed., 33–73. Mexico City: Fondo de Cultura Económica.

Leahy, Margaret

1986   *Development Strategies and the Status of Women: A Comparative Study of the United States, Mexico, the Soviet Union and Cuba.* Boulder: Lynne Rienner.

Lee, Everett

1966   A Theory of Migration. *Demography* 3:47–57.

Lent, John

1979   *Third World Mass Media: Issues, Theory and Research.* Studies in Third World Societies 9. Williamsburg, Va.: Department of Anthropology, College of William and Mary.

LeVine, Sarah

1993   *Dolor y Alegría: Women and Social Change in Urban Mexico.* Madison: University of Wisconsin Press.

Lewis, W. A.

1954   Economic Development with Unlimited Supplies of Labor. *Manchester School of Economic and Social Studies* 5:139–199.

Lomnitz, Larissa, and Marisol Pérez-Lizaur

1987   *A Mexican Elite Family, 1820–1980: Kinship, Class and Culture.* Princeton: Princeton University Press.

Lomnitz-Adler, Claudio
1992   *Exits from the Labyrinth: Culture and Ideology in the Mexican National Space.* Berkeley: University of California Press.

Madsen, William
1973   *Mexican-Americans of South Texas.* New York: Holt, Rinehart and Winston.

Mahler, Sarah
1995   *American Dreaming: Immigrant Life on the Margins.* Princeton: Princeton University Press.

Martínez, Ifigenia
1990   Un proyecto económico alternativo. *Corre la Voz* 52 (November)14–20.

Martínez Gracida, Manuel
1883   Colección de "cuadros sinópticos" de los pueblos, haciendas y ranchos del Estado Líbre y Soberano de Oaxaca. Anexo #50A La Memoria Administrativa Prestada al H. Congreso del Mismo, Oaxaca. Mexico City: Archivo General de la Nación.

Massey, Douglas, Rafael Alarcón, Jorge Durand, and Humberto Gonzales
1987   *Return to Aztlán: The Social Process of International Migration from Western Mexico.* Berkeley: University of California Press.

McCaughan, Edward
1993   Mexico's Long Crisis: Toward New Regimes of Accumulation and Domination. *Latin American Perspectives* 20(3):6–31.

Meillassoux, Claude
[1975] 1981 *Maidens, Meal and Money: Capitalism and the Domestic Community.* Cambridge: Cambridge University Press.

Menchú, Rigoberta
1984   *I, Rigoberta Menchú, An Indian Woman in Guatemala.* London: Verso.

Méndez y Mercado, Leticia Irene
1985   *Migración: decisión involuntaria.* Mexico City: Instituto Nacional Indigenista.

Mills, Nicolaus
1994   *Arguing Immigration: The Debate over the Changing Face of America.* New York: Simon and Schuster.

Mines, Richard
1981   *Developing a Community Tradition: A Field Study in Rural Zacatecas, Mexico and California Settlement Areas.* La Jolla: Program in U.S.–Mexico Studies, University of California, San Diego.

Mines, Richard, and Douglas Massey
1985   Patterns of Migration to the Unites States from Two Mexican Communities. *Latin American Research Review* 20(2):104–123.

Minh-ha, Trinh

1989 *Woman, Native, Other: Writing Postcoloniality and Feminism.* Bloomington: Indiana University Press.

1990 Not You/Like You: Post-Colonial Women and the Interlocking Questions of Identity and Difference. In *Making Face, Making Soul, Haciendo Caras: Creative and Critical Perspectives by Women of Color.* Gloria Anzaldúa, ed., 371–375. San Francisco: Aunt Lute.

1991 *When the Moon Waxes Red: Representation, Gender and Cultural Politics.* New York: Routledge.

Mirande, Alfredo

1988 Chicano fathers: Traditional Perceptions and Current Realities. In *Fatherhood Today.* Phyllis Bronstein and Carolyn Cowan, eds., 93–106. New York: John Wiley.

Mohanty, Chandra

1991 Cartographies of Struggle: Third World Women and the Politics of Feminism. In *Third World Women and the Politics of Feminism.* Chandra Mohanty, Ann Russo, and Lourdes Torres, eds., 1–47. Bloomington: Indiana University Press.

Mohanty, Chandra, Ann Russo, and Lourdes Torres, eds.

1991 *Third World Women and the Politics of Feminism.* Bloomington: Indiana University Press.

Mohar, Alejandro

1992 A Model for the AIDS Epidemic in Mexico: Short-Term Projections. *Journal of Acquired Immune Deficiency Syndromes* 5(3):265–270.

Monsiváis, Carlos

1985 "Landscape, I've Got the Drop on You!" (On the 50th Anniversary of Sound Film in Mexico). *Studies in Latin American Popular Culture* 4:236–249.

Moore, Henrietta

1988 *Feminism and Anthropology.* Minneapolis: University of Minnesota Press.

Mummert, Gail

1988 Mujeres de migrantes y mujeres migrantes de Michoacán: nuevos papeles para las que se quedan y las que se van. In *Movimientos de población en el occidente de México.* Thomas Calvo and Gustavo López, eds., 281–295. Mexico City: El Colegio de Michoacán and Centre d'Études Mexicaines et Centramericaines.

Murillo Castano, Gabriel

1979 *La migración de trabajadores colombianos a Venezuela.* Migraciones Laborales 11. Bogotá: Ministerio de Trabajo y Seguridad Social.

Murphy, Arthur, and Alex Stepick

1991 *Social Inequality in Oaxaca: A History of Resistance and Change.* Philadelphia: Temple University Press.

Nash, June
1980   Aztec Women: The Transition from Status to Class in Empire and Colony. In *Women and Colonization: Anthropological Perspectives.* Mona Etienne and Eleanor Leacock, eds., 134–148. New York: Preager.
1994   Global Integration and Subsistence Insecurity. *American Anthropologist* 96(1):7–30.
1995   The Reassertion of Indigenous Identity: Mayan Responses to State Intervention in Chiapas. *Latin American Research Review* 30(3):7–41.

Oboler, Suzanne
1992   The Politics of Labeling: Latino/a Cultural Identities of Self and Others. *Latin American Perspectives* 19(4):18–36.

Ong, Aihwa
1988   Colonialism and Modernity: Feminist Re-presentations of Women in Non-western Societies. *Inscriptions* 3/4:79–93.

Ornelas López, José Luz
1988   El período cardenista (1934–1940). In *Historia de la cuestión agraria mexicana, Estado de Oaxaca, 1925–1986.* Leticia Reina, ed., 127–188. Mexico City: Juan Pablos Editor, S.A.

Pantojas-García, Emilio
1990   *Development Strategies as Ideology: Puerto Rico's Export-Led Industrialization Experience.* Boulder: Lynne Rienner.

Pastor, Rodolfo
1987   *Campesinos and reformas: La Mixteca, 1700–1856.* Mexico City: El Colegio de México.

Pedraza, Silvia
1991   Women and Migration: The Social Consequences of Gender. *Annual Review of Sociology* 17:303–325.

Peña, Devon
1981   Las Maquiladoras: Mexican Women and Class Struggle in the Border Industries. *Aztlán* 11(2):159–229.

Pessar, Patricia
1982   The Role of Households in International Migration and the Case of U.S.–Bound Migration from the Dominican Republic. *International Migration Review* 16(2):342–364.
1985   The Role of Gender in Dominican Settlement in the United States. In *Women and Change in Latin America.* June Nash and Helen Safa, eds., 273–294. South Hadley, Mass.: Bergin and Garvey.

Portes, Alejandro
1978   Migration and Underdevelopment. *Politics Society* 8(1):1–48.
1989   Latin American Urbanization in the Years of the Crisis. *Latin American Research Review* 24(3):7–44.

Portes, Alejandro, and Jozsef Borocz

1989   Contemporary Immigration: Theoretical Perspectives on Its Determinants and Modes of Incorporation. *International Migration Review* 23(3):606–630.

Portes, Alejandro, and Ruben Rumbaut

1990   *Immigrant America: A Portrait.* Berkeley: University of California Press.

Pronk, Johannes

1993   Migration: The Nomad in Each of Us. *Population and Development Review* 19(2):323–327.

Quintanales, Mirtha

1981   I Paid Very Hard for My Immigrant Ignorance. In *This Bridge Called My Back: Writings by Radical Women of Color.* Cherríe Moraga and Gloria Anzaldúa, eds., 150–156. New York: Kitchen Table, Women of Color Press.

Ramsaran, Ramesh

1992   *The Challenge of Structural Adjustment in the Commonwealth Caribbean.* New York: Praeger.

Rapp, Rayna, Ellen Ross, and Renate Bridenthal

1979   Examining Family History. *Feminist Studies* 5:175–198.

Ravicz, Robert

1965   *Organización social de los mixtecos.* Mexico City: Instituto Nacional Indigenista.

Reding, Andrew, and Christopher Whalen

1991   *Fragile Stability: Reform and Repression in Mexico under Carlos Salinas 1989–1991.* New York: World Policy Institute.

Reichert, Joshua

1981   The Migrant Syndrome: Seasonal U.S. Wage Labor and Rural Development in Central Mexico. *Human Organization* 40(1):56–66.

Riding, Alan

1985   *Distant Neighbors: A Portrait of the Mexicans.* New York: Alfred Knopf.

Roberts, Kenneth

1981   Agrarian Structure and Labor Migration in Rural Mexico. Working Papers in U.S.–Mexican Studies, no. 30. La Jolla: Center for U.S.–Mexican Studies, University of California at San Diego.

Rodríguez Canto, Adolfo, Gabriel Narváez Carvajal, Antonio Hernández Mendo, Jorge Romero Peñaloza, Bernardo Solano Solano, Francisco Dillanes Ramírez, and José de los Santos Castro C.

1989   *Caracterización de la producción agrícola de la región costa de Oaxaca.* Mexico City: Universidad Autónoma Chapingo.

Romero, Mary

1987   Domestic Service in Transition from Rural to Urban Life: The Case of La Chicana. *Women's Studies* 13:199–222.

Romero Frizzi, María de los Angeles
1990   *Economía y vida de los españoles en la Mixteca Alta: 1519–1720.* Mexico City: Instituto Nacional de Antropología e Historia.

Romieu, Isabel, Sonja Sandberg, Alejandro Mohar, and Tamara Awerbuch
1991   Modeling the AIDS epidemic in Mexico City. *Human Biology* 63(5):683–696.

Rosaldo, Renato
1989   *Culture and Truth: The Remaking of Social Analysis.* Boston: Beacon.

Roseberry, William
1989   *Anthropologies and Histories: Essays in Culture, History and Political Economy.* News Brunswick, N.J.: Rutgers University Press.

Rosenbaum, Brenda
1993   *With Our Heads Bowed: The Dynamics of Gender in a Maya Community.* Austin: University of Texas Press.

Rostow, W. W.
1960   *The Stages of Economic Growth.* Cambridge: Cambridge University Press.

Rothstein, Richard
1994   Immigration Dilemmas. In *Arguing Immigration: The Debate over the Changing Face of America.* Nicolaus Mills, ed., 48–63. New York: Simon and Schuster.

Rouse, Roger
1992   Making Sense of Settlement: Class Transformation, Cultural Struggle, and Transnationalism among Mexican Migrants in the United States. In *Towards a Transnational Perspective on Migration: Race, Class, Ethnicity and Nationalism Reconsidered.* Nina Glick Schiller, Linda Basch, and Cristina Blanc-Szanton, eds., 25–52. Annals of the New York Academy of Sciences, vol.645. New York: New York Academy of Sciences.

Ruiz, Vicki, and Susan Tiano, eds.,
1987   *Women on the U.S.–Mexico Border: Responses to Change.* Boston: Allen and Unwin.

Ruiz Cervantes, Francisco José
1988   De la bola a los primeros repartos. In *Historia de la cuestión agraria mexicana, Estado de Oaxaca, prehispánico–1924.* Leticia Reina, ed., 331–423. Mexico City: Juan Pablos Editor, S.A.

Sacks, Karen
1979   *Sisters and Wives: The Past and Future of Sexual Equality.* Urbana: University of Illinois Press.

Salinas de Gortari, Carlos
1982   Political Participation, Public Investment, and Support for the System: A Comparative Study of Rural Communities in Mexico. Research Report Series, no. 35. La Jolla: Center for U.S.–Mexican Studies, University of California at San Diego.
1990   Cinco premisas sobre las relaciones comerciales con el exterior. *Comercio Exterior,* June, 525–526.

Salt, John

1989   A Comparative Overview of International Trends and Types, 1950–80. *International Migration Review* 23(3):431–456.

Sanders, Thomas

1975   Migration from the Mixteca Alta. *North American Series* 3(5):1–16.

Sassen-Koob, Saskia

1978   The International Circulation of Resources and Development: The Case of Migrant Labor. *Development Change* 9:509–545.

1982   Recomposition and Peripheralization at the Core. *Contemporary Marxism* 5:88–100.

Schlesinger, Arthur

1992   *The Disuniting of America.* New York: W.W. Norton.

Scott, James

1985   *Weapons of the Weak: Everyday Forms of Peasant Resistance.* New Haven: Yale University Press.

Segura, Jaime

1988   Los indígenas y los programas de desarrollo agrario (1940–1964). In *Historia de la cuestión agraria mexicana, Estado de Oaxaca, 1925–1986.* Leticia Reina, ed., 189–290. Mexico City: Juan Pablos Editor, S.A.

Selby, Henry, and Arthur Murphy

1982   The Mexican Urban Household and the Decision to Migrate to the U.S. *Occasional Papers in Social Change 4.* Philadelphia: Institute for the Study of Human Issues.

SEP (Secretaría de Educación Pública)

1992   *Mi libro de historia de México,* Cuarto Grado. Mexico City: Secretaría de Educación Pública.

1993   *Libro para el maestro.* Mexico City: Comisión Nacional de los Libros de Texto Gratuitos.

Shorris, Earl

1992   *Latinos: A Biography of the People.* New York: Avon.

Simonelli, Jeanne

1986   *Two Boys, A Girl, and Enough! Reproductive and Economic Decision-Making on the Mexican Periphery.* Boulder: Westview.

Spores, Ronald

1967   *The Mixtec Kings and Their People.* Norman: University of Oklahoma Press.

1984   *The Mixtecs in Ancient and Colonial Times.* Norman: University of Oklahoma Press.

Stabb, Martin

1959   Indigenism and Racism in Mexican Thought: 1857–1911. *Journal of Inter-American Studies* 1(4):405–423.

Stein, Howard
1995   Policy Alternatives to Structural Adjustment in Africa: An Introduction. In *Asian Industrialization and Africa: Studies in Policy Alternatives to Structural Adjustment.* Howard Stein, ed., 1–29. New York: St. Martin's.

Stephen, Lynn
1991   *Zapotec Women.* Austin: University of Texas Press.
1992   Women in Mexico's Popular Movements: Survival Strategies against Ecological and Economic Impoverishment. *Latin American Perspectives* 19(1):73–96.

Stuart, James, and Michael Kearney
1981   Causes and Effects of Agricultural Labor Migration from the Mixteca of Oaxaca to California. Working Papers, no. 28. La Jolla: Center for U.S.–Mexican Studies, University of California at San Diego.

Tangeman, Michael
1995   *Mexico at the Crossroads: Politics, the Church, and the Poor.* Maryknoll, N.Y.: Orbis.

Tibón, Gutierre
[1961] 1984 *Pinotepa Nacional: mixtecos, negros y triques,* 3d ed. Mexico City: Editorial Posada.

Tienda, Marta, and Karen Booth
1991   Gender, Migration and Social Change. *International Sociology* 6(1):51–72.

Todaro, Michael
1976   *Internal Migration in Developing Countries.* Geneva: International Labour Office.

Tomasi, Silvano, Lydio Tomasi, and Mark Miller
1989   Foreward. IMR at 25: Reflections on a Quarter Century of International Migration Research and Orientations for Future Research. *International Migration Review* 23(3):393–402.

Tomlinson, Alan
1990   Introduction: Consumer Culture and the Aura of the Commodity. In *Consumption, Identity and Style: Marketing, Meanings, and the Packaging of Pleasure.* Alan Tomlinson, ed., 1–38. London: Routledge.

Turino, Thomas
1993   *Moving Away from Silence: Music of the Peruvian Altiplano and the Experience of Urban Migration.* Chicago: University of Chicago Press.

Unger, Kurt
1991   Mexican Manufactured Exports and U.S. Transnational Corporations. In *Migration Impacts of Trade and Foreign Investment: Mexico and Caribbean Basin Countries.* Sergio Díaz-Briquets and Sidney Weintraub, eds., 225–254. Boulder: Westview.

U.S. House
1990 Committee on the Judiciary. *Hearings before the Subcommittee on Immigration, Refugees, and International Law.* 101st Cong., 2d. sess. Serial 21. Washington, D.C.: Government Printing Office.

Valdés Rubalcava, Ricardo, ed.
1993 *Oaxaca: tierra del sol.* Mexico City: Secretaría de Educación Pública.

Vallens, Vivian
1978 *Working Women in Mexico during the Porfiriato, 1880–1910.* San Francisco: R&E Research Associates.

Vélez-Ibáñez, Carlos
1983 *Rituals of Marginality: Politics, Process, and Cultural Change in Urban Central Mexico, 1969–1974.* Berkeley: University of California Press.

Villagrán Vázquez, Gabina
1993 Autopercepción de riesgo y uso del condón en estudiantes universitarios mexicanos. *Revista Interamericana de Psicología* 28(1):125–134.

Warman, Arturo
1980 *We Come to Object: The Peasants of Morelos and the National State.* Baltimore: Johns Hopkins Press.

Wells, Alan
1994 The Americanization of Latin American Television. In *Molding the Hearts and Minds: Education, Communications, and Social Change in Latin America.* John Britton, ed., 203–209. Wilmington, Del.: Scholarly Resources.

West, Cornel
1993 *Race Matters.* New York: Vintage.

Williams, Brackette
1989 A Class Act: Anthropology and the Race to Nation across Ethnic Terrain. *Annual Review of Anthropology* 18:401–444.

Williams, Raymond
1958 *Culture and Society, 1780–1950.* London: Chatto and Windus.
1977 *Marxism and Literature.* Oxford: Oxford University Press.
1985 Walking Backwards into the Future. *New Socialist,* May.
1991 Base and Superstructure in Marxist Cultural Theory. In *Rethinking Popular Culture: Contemporary Perspectives in Cultural Studies.* Chandra Mukerji and Michael Schudson, eds., 407–423. Berkeley: University of California Press.

Wilson, Carter
1995 *Hidden in the Blood: A Personal Investigation of AIDS in the Yucatán.* New York: Columbia University Press.

Wolf, Eric
1982 *Europe and the People without History.* Berkeley: University of California Press.

Wood, Charles

1981 Structural Changes and Household Strategies: A Conceptual Framework for the Study of Rural Migration. *Human Organization* 40:338–344.

1982 Equilibrium and Historical-Structural Perspectives on Migration. *International Migration Review* 16(2):98–319.

Woolard, Kathryn

1989 Sentences in the Language Prison: The Rhetorical Structuring of an American Language Policy Debate. *American Ethnologist* 16(2):268–278.

Yeager, Gertrude

1994 Introduction. In *Confronting Change, Challenging Tradition: Women in Latin American History.* Gertrude Yeager, ed., xi–xxi. Wilmington, Del.: Scholarly Resources.

Index

About the Author

Kimberly M. Grimes is an assistant
professor of anthropology at the
University of Delaware in George-
town. She is also the cofounder
and director of Made By Hand
International Cooperative, a non-
profit organization that assists
in the social and economic development of artisan cooperatives
and their communities worldwide
through the advancement of
fair trade practices.